Giacomo Manzù

Giacomo Manzù

JOHN REWALD

NEW YORK GRAPHIC SOCIETY LTD.
GREENWICH, CONNECTICUT

FOR GIULIA AND MILETO

Library of Congress Catalogue Card Number 67-19374

All rights reserved

© 1966 in Austria / Verlag Galerie Welz Salzburg

Printed in Austria

First published in Great Britain 1967 by Thames and Hudson Ltd.

This will certainly not be the last book about Giacomo Manzù, all the more so as he doubtless has many years of artistic creativity in front of him; it must therefore be left to others, at a later date, to honour his work in its entirety. If this book can make any special claim it is that of having been created in completely harmonious co-operation between the sculptor, the publisher and the author. During this friendly co-operation it was not attempted to 'praise the artist with fair words', but rather to present the facts and circumstances relating to his life and work. Our many long conversations, in which Manzù told me of his youth, explained his intentions and elucidated his work and his plans, are recorded here as faithfully as possible. However future generations may interpret his work, on these pages they will find a report which is based on the evidence of the artist and was read by him before appearing in print. The same applies to the illustrations (this is especially important with sculpture, since the lighting and camera angle can easily distort a plastic work). In other words, all those participating strove to achieve an honest and factual publication and at the same time — particularly through the splendid reproductions — to make the work of an outstanding contemporary artist more widely known.

John Rewald

It is one of the eternal wonders of nature that somewhere somebody will be born who — without any recognizable signs — will carry the seed of great artistic creativity. It is not only the parents who are usually amazed by such inexplicable tendencies, but frequently the child itself as well. Gripped by an irresistible urge to create, it will grow up in an atmosphere which is suspicious of, or even antagonistic towards the Muses.

The banker Cézanne of Aix-en-Provence must have remained puzzled to the end of his days by the fact that his only son regarded as his sole mission in life the handling of brushes and paints, an apparently senseless occupation and also one of little financial gain. The grocer Monet of Le Havre probably regarded with equal bewilderment the pictures which reflected the youthful passion of his son. He could not understand why the young man, instead of entering his father's business, was willing to starve in order to paint these unsellable works. Although one can understand why such unexpected tendencies should confound the perplexed parents, the source of these urges, and the reasons why they grip a young man before he himself knows what it means to be an artist, remain inexplicable.

Giacomo Manzù was born on 22 December 1908 in Bergamo. He was the son of a poor cobbler, and the last but one child of the second wife of his father, who lost six of his eleven children in infancy. The poverty-stricken environment in which the child grew up was as remote from any kind of art as was the world of Cézanne the banker. But Bergamo resembles Aix-en-Provence in that both are charming small towns with an abundance of venerable buildings, splendid squares, lovely fountains and medieval streets well suited to capturing a sensitive soul. Such sights, however, usually make a greater impression on the tourist than on a child living in their midst. The boy Giacomo did not, moreover, grow up in historic Bergamo — which crowns the hill — but lived with his family in the new, poor section on the plain which surrounds the jewel of the old town like an ugly setting.

Before he became conscious of its exceptional beauty, the young Manzù was aware of the pronounced devoutness of his home town. Magnificent and solemn processions, mitred bishops and sometimes even cardinals made an ineradicable impression on the child. He may even have seen, without particularly noticing him, a priest from Bergamo, Angelo Roncalli, who was secretary to the local bishop before he became director of the seminary. At an early stage the boy became familiar with Biblical legends and the miracles of many saints, especially local ones; small towns in Catholic countries are much more closely linked with religious traditions than are the great cities.

Bergamo was formerly the northern outpost of the Venetian Republic and the birthplace of Donizetti, as well as of the famous General Colleoni who had a splendid chapel built in 1470 by the architect and sculptor Antonio Amadeo. To this day the town is touched by a breath of ancient glory, serenity and ancestral pride, and it still seems isolated from the plain which it dominates and from neighbouring Lombardy as if it were conscious of its dignity, refusing to demean itself by having contact with less dignified surroundings. Although Milan is now only an hour's drive away, the distance between the towns seems immeasurable. Whereas the big industrial centre has noisily joined the twentieth century, Bergamo cozily suns itself in the quiet charm of the past. When the young Giacomo sometimes climbed into the old part of the town it was as if he had moved into a different world. His childish eyes marvelled at the palaces, churches and towers which his predecessors had raised to the glory of God and themselves. Although he did not feel at ease in these surroundings, for his everyday life was simple and poor, they fired his imagination.

Giacomo's father, who tried his best to feed his large family, was not outstanding in any way, but his mother was a deeply religious and strict woman who always treated the quiet, dreamy boy with indulgence. It is certain that he owes to her his familiarity with the lives of the heroes and martyrs of the Church. His father had a part-time job as sexton of a nunnery with a little church attached, and as such he had a small rent-free apartment. As a child Giacomo often played in the forecourt of the nunnery and also served as an acolyte during the services in the church.

The youth of Manzù passed with the monotony which rules in most impoverished households, where one day is like another and all efforts to make a harsh existence bearable have to be expended. A tired father and sorrowful mother can rarely spend gay and carefree hours with their children, however much they may love them. Giacomo was not a cheerful child. One of his most forceful memories is connected with an event which surpasses in tragedy anything that is normally connected with poverty. After the First World War, when the Spanish influenza epidemic broke out, severely attacking his father and brothers, the ten-year-old helped a sister and a priest to transfer corpses from the hospital to the cemetery. Giacomo carried the cross in front. To strengthen him for his dreary labours, the nurses gave him so much to drink that often on the return journey he fell asleep in a recently emptied coffin. This gruesome experience, as he himself said later, made him so familiar with the sight of unclothed bodies that nudity lost all its mystery for him.

Not all his youthful experiences were so horrendous. Giacomo played, learned and dreamed like other children. But to this day he can remember that, when ten to twelve years old — before he ever thought of classical or modern art — he always dreamed in three dimensions, especially of cubic forms which usually took the shape of high relief. Although he himself cannot recall the details, his sisters maintain that the small Giacomo got himself a severe beating when he stole some clay from a neighbouring Sunday-artist and modelled a full-busted siren with it. We do not know what released his father's anger: Giacomo's dishonest way of getting the material, the fact that the figure was voluptuous, or simply that he had wasted his time with such pursuits. Yet the boy could not be diverted from his purpose; he soon created a series of goats in clay and occasionally begged his sisters and brothers to pose for him, although his ambitions found little response in the family. When he wanted to create a lion he had to be satisfied with the house-cat as a model.

After only a few years of schooling, at the age of eleven, Giacomo had to leave in order to find a job and help maintain the family. As his dexterity and manual ability had been proven beyond doubt, he was apprenticed first to a carpenter and then to a wood-carver. When he was thirteen he went to a gilder and finally to a stucco-worker. The years of apprenticeship gave the boy a splendid opportunity to become familiar with the techniques of various arts. In this manner he acquired the basic knowledge of wood-carving besides learning to work with stone and even crystal. He soon was taught how to handle not only plaster-of-Paris, cement and clay, but also how to construct the armatures for sculpture. The gilder also showed him the various techniques of painting as well as how to prime canvases. At the same time Manzù began to draw, paint and model intensively in his spare time. He naturally did this within the framework of the traditional art which he

8

STANDING GIRL, WITH CHAIR, 1931 Pencil, 17¼ × 12⅝" Owned by the artist

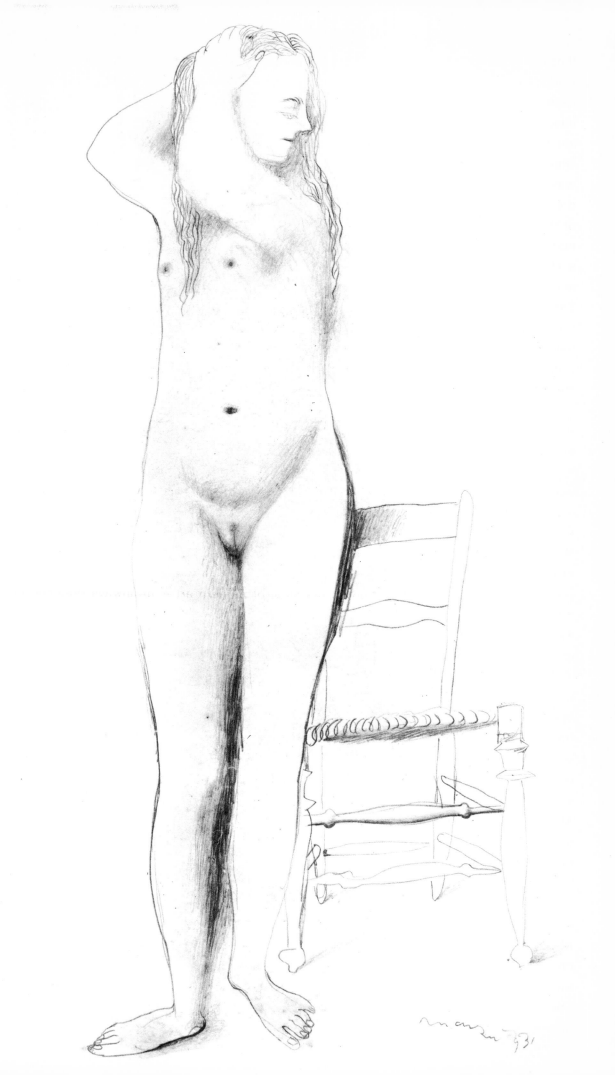

occasionally saw around him. (He knew nothing, at this stage, of the Manifesto of the Futurists which had appeared in Milan in 1910.)

In the meantime the Fascists had come to power. At first they were not antagonistic to the trends of modern art, but they did exclude foreign influences. Bergamo, in any case, remained isolated from all important movements and, as Manzù says today, resembled a small prison which had no contact at all with the spiritual trends of the time. He sometimes came across old art journals, dating from pre-Fascist days, which carried reports about the new tendencies in Paris, or about the Italian masters of the avant-garde such as Carlo Carrà. When he was fifteen he discovered a volume on Aristide Maillol in a bookshop, which he bought with his meagre savings. At that time he knew nothing about modern sculptors and was immediately enraptured by Maillol. For the first time he met a plastic language which discarded whatever was not essential in order to capture the human body in its full roundness, representing it with the utmost simplicity and an innate sense of form. This experience influenced him deeply.

The young man's hunger for stimuli of all kinds could at that time be satisfied only by illustrated books. He reverently studied an illustrated volume about Greece and was especially attracted by the plates showing reliefs. Greek statues seemed more important to him than the works of Donatello — which he also studied from reproductions; a book about Michelangelo equally inspired him.

In some respects Manzù was spared the bitter struggles which Cézanne or Monet had in overcoming their parents' objections. The son of a poor cobbler was not given a choice. It seemed inconceivable that he should ever do anything but follow a modest craft in his home town once his apprenticeship was over. The one thing that was certain was that he would have to stand on his own feet as soon as possible. Since he could not expect any kind of future parental support, it was left to him to decide how to earn his livelihood. If he thought of becoming a sculptor there was only one difficulty; he would have to rely on his own powers, as indeed he would have to do in any profession. Should he wish to spend his spare time in painting or carving there was nothing to stop him. Manzù today considers that his first sketches and projects in many ways resembled the works of Matisse.

The astonishing thing about the slow and tedious education of the young artist is that he found, independently, his way to splendid exemplars despite a lack of any experience or expert guidance. Could he not just as easily have become enthusiastic about the botcheries which were then regarded in Italy — and elsewhere — as sculpture?

The nineteenth century committed many sins against art but its achievements of bad taste in the field of sculpture exceeded anything else. In France Rodin's irresistible force finally banished any mediocrity forever into oblivion. But in Italy there was no one capable of stemming the flood of naked bacchantes, lissome youths, pensive maidens, irate warriors, entwined couples, smiling babes and venerable sages. Even the beautiful impressionistic sculpture in which Medardo Rosso united light and form in a fascinating interplay could not prevail against this. Besides, who had ever heard of Medardo Rosso in Bergamo, although the ageing master had lived in Milan since the war?

At that time Manzù knew nothing of Rosso, who was later to attract him so strongly. His healthy instinct, however, protected him against the atrocities of academic sculpture and against religious k i t s c h. Instead he became engrossed in his book on Maillol; he could not read the French text, but the plates opened his eyes. He knew instinctively what true sculpture was, without having the 'whys and wherefores' explained to him.

It is truly remarkable that Manzù was excited by a living French sculptor, particularly as foreign art has always been neglected in Italy, and especially during the Fascist regime. Italy's own artistic wealth is, of course, overwhelming and she has attracted artists from all countries for centuries past. Perhaps this explains why Italy is the only one among the great art-loving nations which finds almost no space in its museums for the works of foreigners. One can see Poussins in Russia and Goyas in France; Titians and Rembrandts in Germany and Seurats in Holland; Rogier van der Weydens in Madrid; Brueghels in Vienna and Michelangelos in London; but apart from some comparatively rare exceptions, Italy displays only the works of her own artists.

This is a limitation for the younger generation in Italy, however rich the native tradition. Her budding artists can learn about the achievements of other countries only by travel, and very few can afford that. Until recently, before publishers brought out richly illustrated books on art (among which many particularly admirable editions have appeared in Italy), Italians could not even learn about the foreign masterpieces from reproductions, and many artists grew up without knowing what Velasquez, El Greco, Vermeer, Rubens, Hals, Chardin, Delacroix, Manet, Cézanne, Gauguin, van Gogh and numerous others have contributed towards our cultural heritage. Manzù's ingenuousness and ignorance, and his strong need for inspiration, therefore created the basis from which he could see in Maillol's works possibilities for his own.

In 1927 the nineteen-year-old Manzù left Bergamo for the first time to do his military service in Verona. There he discovered the high reliefs of the romanesque bronze doors of San Zeno Maggiore and the equestrian statue of the Can Grande della Scala, the first real masterpieces he saw with his own eyes. He sketched a great deal in his spare time and occasionally attended the Accademia Cignaroli. He also became enthusiastic about photography and purchased a second-hand camera, with which he produced some documentary films; yet he seems to have abandoned, fairly quickly, his dream of becoming a film director. Medardo Rosso died in 1928; Manzù, who had not yet begun to value his work, thus never had a chance to meet him. In the meanwhile he had started to model regularly. His first plastic works were tinted. Today he cannot understand how these early, coloured works, executed almost in the manner of the early Greeks, came into being. His wish to become a sculptor became more urgent, and since his mother had died in the same year, he decided not to return to Bergamo when his eighteen months of military service were over, but to go to Paris instead. Naturally he dreamed of meeting Maillol there.

FIRST STAY IN PARIS

Despite the fact that Manzù had seen very little of the artistic life of Italy, he longed to breathe a fresher air, where a crippling academic tradition did not threaten to smother any new movement in embryo. By the end of 1928, the twenty-year-old artist went to Paris with a friend (a waiter by profession) whom he promptly lost sight of on arrival. Manzù intended to work for one or two years in order to earn his livelihood, and then to dedicate himself to sculpture. Since he had no working permit he found it impossible to obtain employment. Aimlessly he roamed the wintry streets, and when his money gave out he had to stop eating altogether. He went to the Louvre only once, but hunger prevented him from truly appreciating any of the masterpieces there. He never went to the Rodin Museum at all, and his hopes of visiting Maillol came to nothing. After surviving for twenty days with practically no nourishment, Manzù collapsed in the street. As a distressed, and hence suspicious, foreigner he was arrested and turned over to his consulate, which bundled him home. At the border he was met by the Fascist police who accompanied him to Milan and confiscated his passport.

Although Manzù's first attempt to obtain some schooling in his own way had gone sadly

WOMAN COMBING HER HAIR, 1932
Pencil, 17⅝ × 11⅞"
Coll. Arturo Brivec, Bergamo

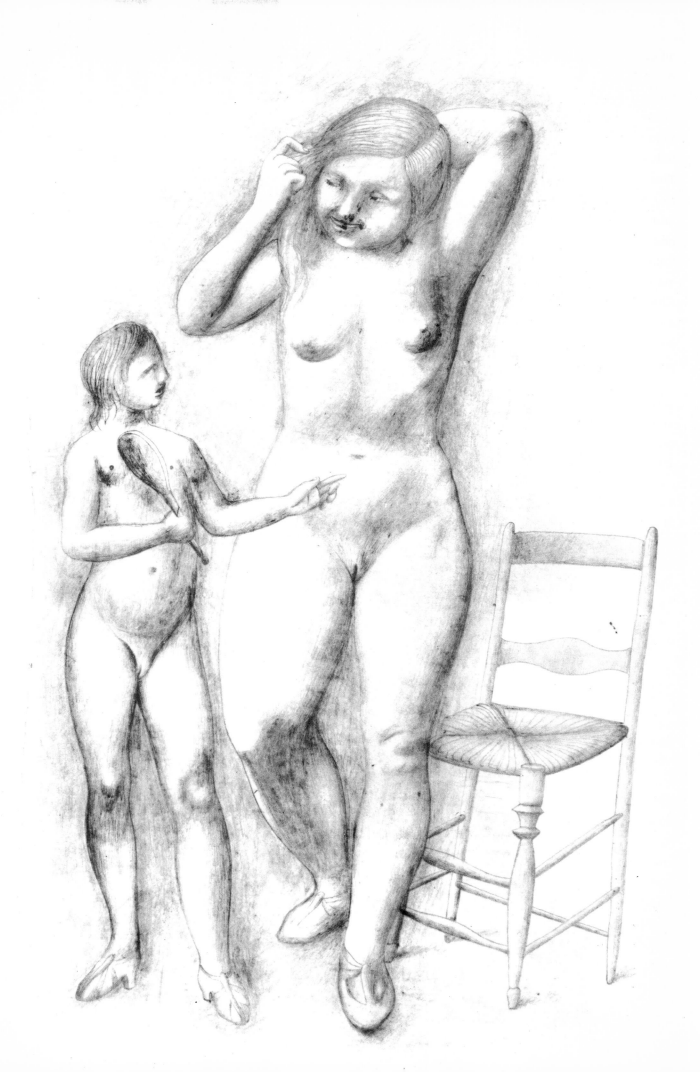

astray, his determination to become an artist had not weakened. He was now forced to develop his gifts without any stimulation from Paris — where daring novelties were constantly attempted — and at the same time to fight against the most grinding poverty, which usually opposes with malevolent obduracy the development of diffident talents.

Despite the rashness of his expedition to Paris Manzù was not foolhardy; what he lacked in adventurousness and youthful high spirits he made up for by a tenacious will to let nothing stand in his way. He felt an irresistible desire to devote his life exclusively to creative art, probably without himself knowing the source of his inner strength. Since he had always known the tribulations of everyday life, and was only too familiar with hunger, no external circumstances could divert him from his purpose. He was perfectly willing to make the necessary sacrifices to the powers that inspired him. In any case Milan offered him more opportunities than Bergamo to maintain himself somehow or other.

FIRST IMPORTANT SCULPTURES

Manzù luckily received his first commission through Muzio, an architect friend: the decoration of a chapel of the Catholic University for which he made some saints and ornamental figures. This gave him a chance to work with cement, plaster, stone and metal. He asked to be paid a modest weekly wage. A cellar or a garage served as his studio and there — besides the works for the chapel — his first important sculptures came into being. They were mainly coloured and naturalistic, as for instance a reclining figure in clay, a guitar player in coloured cement, a painted plaster relief of Adam and Eve and an almost life-size Sulamith in tinted cement. These pieces were created from imagination since he could not afford professional models, but friends and their female companions often posed for his numerous sketches. In 1930 he began to paint occasionally, and in the same year took part in a small group exhibition in a Milan gallery. He showed two portrait heads and a series of drawings. From time to time he even sold something.

In the following year he created a coloured stucco relief of an 'Annunciation', a tinted terra-cotta of a 'Gatekeeper' and a 'Pillar of Solomon' in marble, his first work in stone. These early pieces betray the search for a personal expression, Manzù often harking back to the Etruscans or the work of thirteenth-century stone-masons. While occasionally using colour in a completely abstract way, he simultaneously showed an almost brutal realism in works like the 'Gatekeeper'; in the relief of the 'Annunciation', on the other hand, he aspired to a lyrical expression, and was successful despite a certain clumsiness. By 1932 this clumsiness of the tyro was beginning to give place to a much more skilful arrangement of the various planes of relief. There now appears a tendency towards stylization, however, as for instance in a circus scene, which clearly shows the dangers to which an artist is exposed if, at an early stage, he commands an extraordinary dexterity.

Today Manzù considers the years 1930–3 as his primitive period, in which his sculptures were influenced by early Christian art, while in his drawings he succumbed, as he himself admits, to certain mannerisms.

It is notable that Manzù had from the start a particular predilection for two diametrically opposed types of subjects, and that he remained true to them later: aspects of everyday life on the one hand, and scenes from the Bible on the other. These two main groups of his work were soon supplemented, however, when female nudes and portrait heads began to play a predominant role. According to a friend of his youth, Manzù read the Bible a great deal in Milan, especially the Song of Solomon, which stimulated him to mystic dreams. Biblical events always preoccupied the artist to an extraordinary extent.

The piety of his mother may have made a lasting impression, but the tales of the Old and New Testaments probably stimulated him directly towards plastic expression. He found in them attractive episodes particularly suited for representation in reliefs, in which several figures could be united. That he depicted Biblical themes so frequently and so gladly is not so much connected with his own religious convictions, as with the fact that this was a world with which he had been familiar since childhood. There he found subjects which he could not only grasp emotionally but also visualize with immediacy; they took shape in front of his eyes, so to speak.

During his stay in Milan Manzù came into contact with a number of more or less similarly minded young painters, sculptors, authors, art critics and poets; in their company he could at last discuss many burning questions about art and life. He no longer felt quite so lonely and gradually realized that new forces were at work whose unified spirit had to triumph one day. It is self-evident that Mussolini did not have many adherents in these 'Sturm-und-Drang' circles.

Since Manzù was solitary by nature, lively debates in a circle of friends could not quench his thirst for knowledge, although they were of great value in sharpening his mind. He went to public libraries in order to read and absorb more of modern culture. While his knowledge of Maillol's work was still confined to illustrations, the works of Medardo Rosso and the curiously restrained and yet penetrating sculpture of Ernesto di Fiori began to have a lasting influence on him.

Manzù's father died in 1932. The artist again took part in a group exhibition at the Gallerie del Milione, and his contributions for the first time attracted the notice of the press. He continued to work on low reliefs with religious themes which he chased in copper. He also painted a great deal and occasionally tried his hand at etching. In 1933 he created the first version of an important statue, the idea for which originated in 1931. At that time Manzù had made seven sketches of the daughter of a friend, a ten- or eleven-year-old child who sat naked on a slender, rush-bottomed chair. This chair, which the sculptor had brought with him from Bergamo almost as a fetish, does not appear in the first life-size version chased in copper. The sculptor regarded it merely as a preparation, to be followed by further studies and other, more elaborate versions. It is typical of Manzù's method of working that a long time may often elapse before his ideas take shape, and that they may then occupy him for years. He constantly goes back to a given subject, alters its form and develops it further. Withal he usually works from imagination and without a model; frequently — as in this case — he is satisfied with a small number of sketches.

Despite his intensive activity Manzù apparently could not get used to the rigours of city life; around 1933–4 he decided to leave Milan. He retired to Bergamo for a full year and passed the time without doing much work. He seems to have needed this breathing spell in solitude to master the new impressions and events. He looked at has own creations with unusually critical eyes, and destroyed a number of works made since 1929 which no longer satisfied his standards. In later years the artist repeated such auto-da-fés from time to time; even his best friends or clamouring customers could not prevent the destruction of discarded drawings, clay models and even bronze casts.

In January 1934 Manzù went to Rome, where he could see and study Greek sculpture for the first time. During his short stay he also saw, while visiting St Peter's, the pope enthroned between two seated cardinals. This solemn group recalled many youthful memories and was to leave a permanent impression. But in Manzù's characteristic way

16

there was a gap of several years before the unusual forms of the cardinals found artistic expression. One might think that he does not trust spontaneous impressions or does not want to give way to them, preferring to carry them around for a long time before coming to grips with them. Although Manzù can still vividly recall that meeting with the seated cardinals, which brought his childhood back to his mind's eye, he did not execute his first sculpture of a cardinal until two years later. Despite the long period of incubation this first work was a failure and was destroyed. Perhaps he had not yet given sufficient inner concern to the theme to find a valid form for it. But it is more probable that the prolonged brooding had created such a wealth of plastic conceptions and ideas that they stood in the way of the first practical execution. In fact the sculptor subsequently created a series of over fifty figures of cardinals, until he felt that the possibilities of this subject had become exhausted.

The year 1934 was eventful for Manzù. He returned to Milan and married a Milanese girl. His wife did not have a great understanding of his aims, however, and he had to carry on working in comparative solitude, but she was prepared to share his impoverished existence and also to serve him as a model. The next year she bore a daughter, followed in 1937 by another girl and by a son, Pio, in 1939.

The artist remembers 1934 mainly as a critical period, which is certainly connected with a change in style that took place at that time. Although Manzù likes to ponder a great deal he is no philosopher and he did not, by any means, return to Milan from his year of exile in Bergamo with new theories of art. Nevertheless, his self-imposed period of rest had served to rid him of a certain beginner's clumsiness, and helped him to turn his back — consciously or unconsciously — on all stylization in order to hold closer to observations from nature. He did this with a series of feminine heads, some of them of his young wife.

Manzù freely admits to having succumbed to the influence of Medardo Rosso during this important phase. This is not really surprising if one considers that he had no academic training on the one hand, and did not feel attracted to the newer and more radical movements in art — for instance, Italian futurism — on the other. In such circumstances it seems thoroughly logical for the young artist, torn with doubts and hopes, to see Rosso's example as a means of escape not only from k i t s c h, but also from the avant-garde. What Manzù discovered in Rosso was a soulful interpretation of natural forms, often abandoning details so as to let the light play around broadly conceived masses, and thus constantly creating new effects. Rosso had gone further in his efforts to simplify volumes than Manzù himself intended to go, so that the younger man may have felt towards Rosso's work what Maillol felt for Rodin's statues, namely the wish to bring a more solid and calmer expression to the loosened and frequently dramatic forms of his predecessor. But Manzù owes to Rosso the realization that there is a special virtue and power in simplicity, and that the impression of movement can be created by suggestion, without the necessity of representing it literally. In addition to this Rosso gave him an example of how to enliven planes, insofar as his material — usually wax — was handled with such mastery that there are no 'dead', or even neutral, areas anywhere. The more summarily the forms of Medardo Rosso are conceived, the more lively are the surfaces, and the apparently fortuitous irregularities, to which light seems to cling, always exert new charms. In contrast to the academic sculptors of his time, Rosso realized that a sculpture is not composed of a series of 'profiles' which are connected to each other by the medium, but that plastic works consist of rounded bodies, the smallest element of which plays a part in the tension and expressivity of the whole.

The difference between a pebble and a piece of sculpture, both of them three-dimensional, is that behind the sculpture lies a concept, a creative will. When this concept is valid, when it poses and solves a specific problem (rather than avoiding it), and when the execution follows the concept with a more or less irresistible impulse, a work of art is born. Manzù, who was then almost thirty years old, was doubtless filled with such energies; these at first manifested themselves in a series of portrait heads.

The relationship of these heads to the works of Rosso is particularly obvious because Manzù sometimes even used Rosso's favourite medium — wax. But despite this the young sculptor managed to achieve a personal style, which discarded the frequently complacent virtuosity of Rosso, being satisfied with simpler forms and a more restrained expression. Manzù's early portraits are penetratingly observed and executed with great delicacy. The lively, usually spontaneously kneaded structure of Rosso's surfaces is replaced by a more deliberate technique. It is precisely the great modesty and unpretentiousness of these heads which reflects the self-willed character of Manzù, who determinedly kept away from all modern trends with matter-of-fact certainty, tried to link up with the past and avoided all cheap effects in order to create directly what he considered beautiful and important. Manzù worked with loving care but without sentimentality. He succeed in capturing his models so completely without ever underlining any special feature (much less resorting to the distortions of caricature) that the viewer is not only convinced of the likeness of his portraits but at the same time gets the feeling that the artist has surprised and held the most essential expression.

These unusual attributes, the absence of all concern with theoretical problems in favour of a natural pleasure in classical harmonies, were probably the reason for the artist's initial successes. Daily existence was still difficult and his first bronzes had to be cast on credit, but nevertheless he appeared more frequently in group exhibitions, was increasingly noticed by the press and enjoyed an occasional sale. This increased his will to work and gave him sufficient self-confidence to renew his connections with Milan's intellectual circles, with which he had already been in contact during his previous stay.

The young artists and writers who often met, openly or secretly, in Milan (the industrial capital of Italy) belonged to the élite of the country. They were no longer content to be merely anti-Fascist; most of them were practising Communists. In the meantime Hitler had seized power in Germany and the Spanish Civil War was in the offing, so that the fight against dictatorship had to be waged on an international basis, openly supported only by Soviet Russia. Theoreticians and agitators, adventurers and idealists who were prepared to risk their lives, came together in groups to struggle for the destruction of tyranny and to plan the preparation of a better future. Although Manzù did not become a member of the Communist party, he largely shared the opinions of his comrades.

The political r a p p r o c h e m e n t with Russia, probably inevitable under the given circumstances, was accompanied by contradictions to which little attention seems to have been paid at the time. The so-called 'cult of personality', for instance, was practised as boundlessly in Moscow as in Berlin or Rome; this seems completely to have escaped the young anti-Fascists (they of course had never even heard of a 'personality cult' before the Kremlin coined the phrase with retrospective meaning). Nor does it seem to have bothered these frequently fanatical intellectuals that Stalin — rather like Hitler — was far more reactionary and impatient in questions of art and culture than Mussolini. It appears almost incomprehensible that the Communist artists of Italy could have defended the Russian 'cultural line'. But then they perhaps closed their eyes to anything that had no direct connection with political aims, i. e. the fight for liberation.

20 Apart from politics the main subject of discussion was naturally art. There is probably no

RECLINING WOMAN, 1940
Pen and ink, 8½×15''
Coll. Pio Manzoni, Bergamo

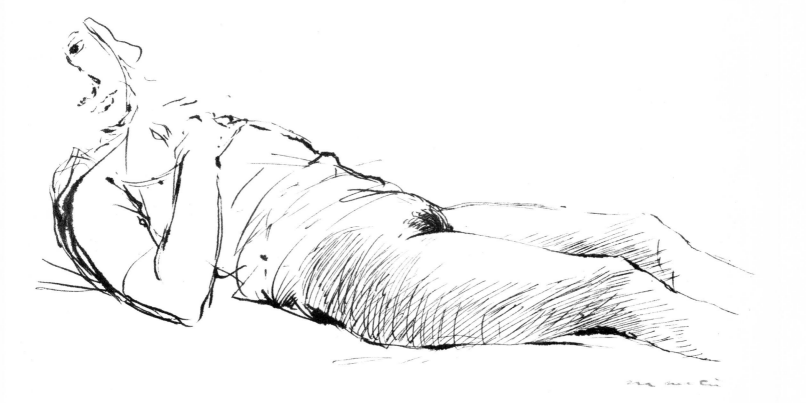

STUDY FOR SUSANNA, 1940
Ink wash, 10¼ × 15"
Coll. Pio Manzoni, Bergamo

STUDY FOR SUSANNA, 1944
Sepia wash, $10\frac{1}{4} \times 15$"
Coll. Pio Manzoni, Bergamo

MOTHER AND CHILD, c. 1946
Black chalk with watercolour

other country in which the opinions of art critics are so passionately debated, or where the rivalries of opposing colleagues are followed with as much partiality as in Italy. Every writer on art has adherents and enemies who pounce on his utterances as if they were of world-shaking importance. In most studios there is a tense expectancy to discover what this or that commentator has to say about an exhibition, although the views of the oracle are usually known in advance and merely the degree of his rejection or rapture remains in question. Each word is weighed and interpreted with hatred or delight, disgust or reverence, which is all the more productive as these words — unless they resemble clarion calls — are often chosen with acrobatic flexibility.

The art critics are naturally conscious of the unusual power of their dicta and cannot always avoid the conceit that it is their contribution which endows cultural events with their true significance. This curious state of affairs would be quite harmless if the artists themselves did not lend so much importance to it. The formation of cliques is dangerous only because the artists are thus divided into clans with the result, for instance, that praise from one quarter will automatically release disapprobation from another.

Manzù kept away from this nuisance as far as possible. This was due not so much to calculation as to a certain peasant's wiliness which prevented him from being tied in any way, not to speak of his natural dislike of theoretical expositions and aesthetic interpretations. Since he considers himself an artist and not an intellectual, he instinctively avoids disputations which tend to become metaphysical. Just as he had joined his Communist colleagues without becoming a party member and without relinquishing his religious themes, so he also avoided involvement with individual artistic groups, especially as his work springs from a creative obsession rather than from philosophical or political opinions. He did not then, and does not now, belong among those artists who attach much importance to the speculative interpretation of their intentions.

Although Manzù is quite conscious of his importance as a sculptor (a feeling that has naturally been strengthened by his increasing success), this realization could not overcome his inborn shyness; it merely served to liberate him a little from his uncertainty and timidity. His restraint nowadays hides the dignity of a man who knows himself confirmed by life. At the same time a sense of humour and an almost childish tendency to joyous or astonished outbursts have preserved him from all solemn pompositiy. However, his reactions are by no means primitive, and, despite his modest demeanour, one feels in his presence that he is a man keenly aware, through extraordinarily sensitive antennae, of what the surrounding world can offer. His eyes search and scrutinize the people around him, objects which fascinate him, young girls he meets in the street and children he notices in passing. All that he sees is silently committed to his visual memory.

While less articulate than the Sicilian painter Renato Guttuso, with whom he made friends in Milan, Manzù is by no means clumsy of speech though he usually prefers to enter a debate only in order to correct an opinion he considers fallacious. The sculptor, who has up to then been thoughtful and quiet, suddenly comes to life and his voice rings with passionate conviction. It is quite clear that he does not participate in a conversation just to hear his own voice but to defend a point of view close to his heart. Yet since this happens rarely and since he avoids all rhetorical embroidery, he is usually listened to in attentive silence which lends his words all the more weight. But as soon as Manzù has explained his viewpoint, he withdraws again into the role of a silent participant who follows the temperamental digressions of his colleagues with an occasional firm nod of agreement or a half-suppressed smile.

Even when receiving friends in his own studio, Manzù will not be drawn into long explanations. He usually shows his works without any comment, at the most giving some technical information, while his eyes roam distractedly over the scattered statues. His silence, however, is not a demand for approval; if a visitor expresses boundless admiration for a specific work it may happen that the artist, somewhat embarrassed, quite unsentimentally admits to not being completely satisfied with that particular piece which he will probably destroy. Some of the sculptures from this period in Milan also became victims of his disapproval.

In 1934 Manzù returned to low relief which, in his own words, attracts him because it offers opportunities related to painting; it also gives him the chance to assemble forms on a plane which is at the same time a space of limited depth. This forces him to tackle questions of spatial relationship. Since reliefs mainly pose the problem of plastic bodies set against a background, they differ fundamentally from self-sufficient sculptures in the round which need not consider relationship to other objects or planes. Although the art of relief is one of the greatest achievements of Italian art (without detracting in any way from the Greeks) it had been lost in the recent past, so that Manzù was practically left to himself in his efforts to reconnect with this tradition.

Manzù likes to draw parallels between painting and reliefs — since in both, spatial depth must be created by means of an illusion — yet his development (with the exception of a series of high reliefs) gradually drew him away from pictorial compositions with their interplay of light and shade and led him slowly to a much flatter conception of the relief. His low reliefs no longer have anything in common with painting; one could regard them as drawings without colour to which gently swelling forms have been added. However, several years passed before the artist managed to find a distinctive style in this field.

In 1934, for the first time, the work of Manzù was shown outside Italy when he participated in a group exhibition in St Gallen. In the following year he was represented in a show of old and modern Italian art in Paris and, in 1936, his sculptures were exhibited in Budapest with other contemporary Italian works. In the same year a short visit of fourteen days took him once more to Paris.

SECOND STAY IN PARIS

Manzù's second stay in Paris was much happier than his adventure of 1929. This time he could visit the Louvre at his leisure to study the pictures of the impressionists, which he had previously known only by hearsay and of which the works of the Italian Macchiaioli had given him only a vague idea. Manzù was especially taken with Renoir, Cézanne and Seurat but he did not neglect the old masters, among whom Caravaggio and Leonardo da Vinci interested him particularly. He was also deeply impressed by the sculpture of the Egyptians and Greeks in the Louvre. Of equal importance to him was the Rodin Museum. (Translations of Italian biographies of Manzù, according to which the sculptor met Rodin on this journey to Paris, are obviously misleading; since the Frenchman died in 1917 the 'meeting' can only have been onesided.) Manzù was not especially enthusiastic about the large important bronzes of Rodin but more taken with the small statuettes and studies in clay which are not as well known, but in which the hand of the master is directly visible. They maintain the master's spontaneity, which is usually lost in the more pretentious pieces. Manzù, who himself wrestles for years with the conception of an idea, could not withstand the charm of these little figures which a genius in the overflowing bounty of his gifts had kneaded almost as a side-line.

26

GENERAL, 1941
Study for a relief of the
Crucifixion series
Pencil and red ink, 13×6½"
Galerie Welz, Salzburg

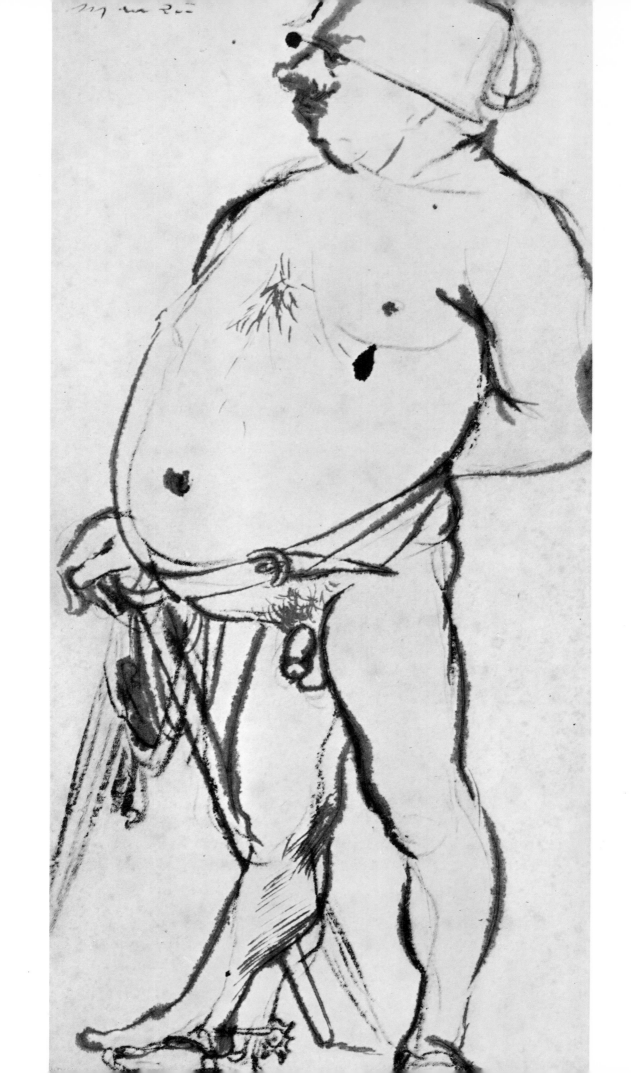

His stay in Paris was so short that Manzù had no opportunity to visit Maillol. Besides, his interest in this artist had waned since his own work had begun to lead him in a different direction. He now felt more attracted to radical pioneers like Picasso, Matisse and Braque.

Paris offered Manzù the first opportunity to become acquainted with the avant-garde of which, despite the fact that Milan was Italy's most progressive town, he had heard only a faint echo. Here he saw the works of Brancusi which unexpectedly impressed him greatly. He also became acquainted with the plastic works of two painters, Renoir and Picasso, of which he had not been aware previously. On the other hand Manzù cannot recall when he first saw the bronzes of Degas; in any case they made little impression on him.

Manzù made no personal contacts with Parisian artists. He had too much respect for the various masters to attempt to approach them, especially as he was still completely unknown in Paris. The French attitude is less chauvinistic than the Italian one and permits foreigners to achieve renown, provided they live in France and thus belong to the 'Ecole de Paris'. Those who do not fall within the wide framework of this school (like Munch, Klee, Mondrian or Kokoschka) must be more or less resigned to finding little and slow recognition in Paris. The Italian contribution to this cosmopolitan school having been comparatively small since the death of Modigliani, Manzù found hardly any compatriots who could have introduced him into the local art circles.

Despite frantic activity the French art life was then at a critical point. Most of the fauves who had been so promising at the turn of the century had become weak in the meantime, for instance Derain, Dufy, Vlaminck and van Dongen. Cubism, which Manzù had quickly learned to admire, had long ceased to be an active force, even though it survived in the sculpture of Laurens and Gonzales. André Breton tried to keep surrealism, the last group movement on the Paris scene, alive by all manner of means. As a matter of fact the artistic reality consisted only of a few 'old masters' such as Matisse, Bonnard, Rouault and Braque, who nearly all lived and worked in isolation. Among the sculptors, besides the ageing Maillol and Despiau, a few younger men such as Zadkine or Lipchitz occasionally attracted notice.

At that time Paris was preparing for the World's Fair of 1937, for which a rather ugly Museum of Modern Art was being erected, overwhelmingly decorated with meaningless statues and reliefs. At that exhibition Nazi Germany and the Soviet Union were to manifest their claims to leadership through gigantic, pompous statues, which vied with each other in vulgarity.

Whereas Manzù's first 'pilgrimage' to Paris might have become a turning point in the development of the sculptor, his second one left no discernible traces. Influences are effectual only when a questing or dissatisfied artist meets stimuli which promise solutions to his problems or direct him to strike out along a new line. By 1936 Manzù was no longer in such a position; he had already discovered a form of beauty that inspired him, even if it did not yet find complete expression in his works. Above all he felt himself too closely connected with nature to receive inspiration from the Paris school which was engaged in reshaping nature more or less drastically. While he admired the purity and perfection of Brancusi's creations, this did not mean that they would henceforth serve as models for his own work. Manzù was not even perplexed by the manifold trends he found in Paris; if anything, they confirmed his personal conviction which now, as never before, seemed in harmony with his innermost being.

Manzù thus continued to seek an individual style without breaking with classical tradition. Instead of being enticed into experiments like so many others, and instead of striving for a new world of forms and contents, he was satisfied with the less pretentious task of expressing the tenderness of his emotions in harmonic lines, gently treated surfaces and balanced forms. At a time when anything 'new' was a prerequisite for success on the one hand, and traditions were used mostly to justify sentimental botches on the other, it required great courage to reject any compromise with the so-called contemporary taste and, in a simple and modest fashion, remain true to oneself. This explains why Manzù's second visit to France was not followed by any noticeable change in his style; it merely represented a short escape from the oppressive atmosphere of Fascism. In Paris he could breathe fresh air and make acquaintance — albeit fleeting — with the activity of the centre of modern art.

Manzù used his few days in Paris to make some political contacts. He and his friend, the Milan painter Aligi Sassù, who accompanied him throughout the trip, set out for the journey home provided with anti-Fascist literature. When the train approached the Italian border, the two artists began to feel uneasy. This did not escape the notice of a Catholic priest travelling in the same compartment. He kindly offered his help and the brochures were safely smuggled across the border under his soutane.

Manzù continued his work in Milan. His first version of a cardinal, subsequently destroyed, dates from this period. In 1937 the artist suffered one of the hardest blows of fate. His two-year-old daughter died; he did not have the means to provide her with the care which might possibly have saved her.

FIRST ONE-MAN EXHIBITION IN ROME

After the death of his child, Manzù went to Rome for two months in February 1937, in order to divert his thoughts. In March, the small Galleria della Cometa held his first one-man exhibition there, for which Carlo Carrà, one of the founders of futurism, wrote the introduction. The show was a great success and particularly important to the artist, for it made him known in the capital of his country. He also met there Carlo Ragghianti and Cesare Brandi, two art critics with whom he has remained in close touch ever since. While he was in Rome all his friends among the Milan artists and writers, including Sassù, were arrested as Communists. Manzù had ammunition hidden in his cellar, which the police failed to discover during the two searches they made of his house. Nevertheless, due to his absence, the sculptor escaped almost certain arrest which could have resulted in imprisonment for many years, as indeed it did for several members of his circle.

After Manzù's return from Rome, his wife bore a second daughter, who died only six months later. Manzù was devastated; he continued his work, not so much to find consolation but rather to avoid unbearable brooding. Among the works of this year is a small high relief which for the first time treats the theme of the artist and his model, two years after some etchings had been devoted to the same subject. The sculptor repeatedly returned to his theme and five years later treated it on a large scale. Simultaneously he was also occupied with a similar subject, a self-portrait with model, the first relief of which dated from 1936. In both cases the composition deals with a man, usually clothed, opposite a nude woman; a grouping which Manzù has continued to depict up to the present day in numerous drawings, gouaches and oils. At the same time he now returned to the project of the naked, sitting child, which had preoccupied him since 1931. This first sculpture was only twenty inches high, and the chair was cast separately. The casting was in lead. Manzù did not complete the first life-size version of this series until a full ten years later.

SEATED WOMAN, 1946
Pen and ink, 13⅝×9⅝"

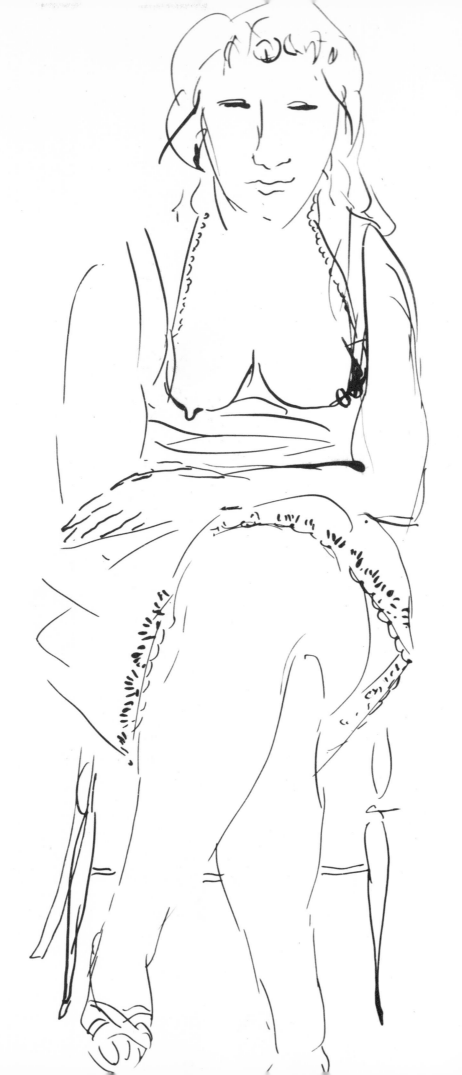

Manzù

disegno 1943

Among the nudes which became increasingly frequent in Manzù's works, is a 'Susanna' in wax. Its unrestrained, crouching position foreshadows later pieces in which arms lying close to the body and drawn-up knees create comparatively compact masses which, through sensitive modelling, attain their inner articulation. In some details the treatment even resembles reliefs, for instance in the way the arm lying between the breasts and the hand nestling against the shoulder, seem to melt into the body yet maintain their own form.

In the following year Manzù created a 'David', which may recall the earlier 'Gatekeeper' in its harsh realism, although the problem of the squatting child is here solved with an amazing sureness. A number of extremely tender portraits of women provide, perhaps for the last time, a memory of Medardo Rosso, and a three foot high cardinal, executed in the summer of 1938, constitutes the first surviving version of the future series. The artist was now thirty years old and in the process of unfolding his innate talent as well as his acquired knowledge. At the Biennale of Venice in 1938 his works won him a success of great promise.

THE SERIES OF RELIEFS: 'CRISTO NELLA NOSTRA UMANITA'

There appears a break in Manzù's work between 1938 and 1939, because during this period he was almost exclusively employed on a series of eight reliefs: 'Cristo nella nostra umanità'. Hitler had just won his last bloodless victory at Munich, in which Mussolini had to be content with a subordinate role. Only incurable optimists still believed in a peaceful solution to the threatening conflict. Driven by his own tragedy and by dark premonitions, Manzù worked on religious themes which, as in the days of the German Reformation, were at the same time a pretext for political commentary. It seems as if the taciturn, modest and restrained artist could no longer repress the accumulation of bitterness and indignation. Most of his friends were in prison; the Fascist press was becoming increasingly aggressive; the radio shouted challenges; the world seemed to be drifting towards an unimaginable catastrophe . . . Was this the time to devote oneself to gracious portraits of smiling women and nude studies of young girls? But Manzù was an artist, not a polemicist; his protest had to be in a creative field.

Manzù's new reliefs mostly represented the crucified Jesus or the Descent from the Cross. He found in them the perfect way of fashioning forms against a flat background which he had dreamed of for so long. The bodies hardly rise from the plane, but gentle modelling — to which are added here and there some boldly sketched lines — gives them an amazing plasticity. Although the figures are still isolated and seldom intersect, and although there are practically no indications of perspective, an astonishing illusion of space is created. On top of this the accents of the composition are distributed in so masterly a fashion that the relationship of empty zones, and the single figures which detach themselves from these, create a further element of drama and suggested depth. The artist largely dispensed with detail and in some cases did not even indicate the cross, contenting himself with an almost floating Christ with outstretched arms and lowered head, without however weakening the expression of eternal agony. Since the crown of thorns is also missing, the crucified one (who in some of these reliefs, incidentally, hangs by one arm which is nailed or bound to the cross) seems to be nothing more nor less than a symbol of human suffering. While believers will unmistakeably recognize the Son of God, others may think of a strung-up anti-Fascist.

The slender, youthful body of the Crucified is surrounded by the naked figures of weeping prostitutes and coarse soldiers. A fat fellow with a lance wears a German steel helmet of the First World War; an equally naked, bloated general catches the eye because of his headgear, which suspiciously resembles a chamber pot decorated with a swastika. Beside one cross, on which a grinning skeleton is suspended, stands a bareheaded old man carrying a mitre in his hands. But at no point do these allusions turn into caricature. On the contrary, the tenderness of execution, the harmonic grouping of the figures and the lack of any kind of action withdraw all appearance of passionate rebellion from these reliefs. The protest embodied in them is silent, yet this does not by any means indicate that it lacks penetration.

In his woodcuts of the Apocalypse, Dürer depicted some cardinals and even popes among those damned on Judgment Day, thus indicating that he was in agreement with Luther's attacks on the infallability of the Holy See. In the same way Manzù represented the martyrdom of Jesus not as an historical event, but showed it in the light of the present day, in which helpless men were again tortured and killed because of their convictions. The manner in which Manzù drew these parallels was mild compared to what was to happen in the near future. While the artist was working on the reliefs, Hitler, in the autumn of 1939, overran Poland, and Stalin soon appropriated his portion of it. The Third Reich and the Kremlin had become allies, whereas the daring conqueror of Abyssinia and Albania still played a waiting game.

PROFESSOR IN MILAN AND TURIN

In 1940 Manzù and his friend Carrà were nominated as professors at the Brera in Milan, together with Marino Marini and Felice Casorati. Manzù was, however, almost at once 'lent' to the Academy of Turin as teacher of sculpture. He had barely taken up his post when Hitler broke through the Maginot line and penetrated deep into France. Mussolini could not resist the temptation to pounce on the helpless country and make certain of his share of the loot. As a professor in a government school Manzù avoided conscription into the Italian army.

The artist conscientiously applied himself to advising young people in that which he himself had acquired so laboriously. Although this meant sacrificing some of his time and his work, he found a deep satisfaction in teaching. He was fully conscious of the fact that it is impossible to transmit to others 'how to make a beautiful statue', but he could at least show them 'what to do to avoid making a bad sculpture'. He naturally did not confine himself to purely technical questions, but tried above all to kindle in his pupils a true devotion to their art and a sincere love of nature.

Since Manzù himself can only work in the silence and solitude of his studio, he could not carry on his own work during his teaching periods. Nevertheless some important statues date from that time, including a small sitting cardinal in bronze, the rhythmic folds of whose ample vestments were to determine the future series of cardinals. Some feminine busts of this period are remarkable because of a much livelier technique, which is also reflected in the first relief of a self-portrait with model. But the artist was mainly occupied with continuing his series of reliefs on the theme of Christ's death. The first group of these, created in 1939 and in the meantime cast in bronze, was exhibited in the Galleria Barbaroux in Milan in the spring of 1941.

It was undoubtedly daring to exhibit these works — castigating the crimes of those

PAINTER AND MODEL, 1
Pastel and gouache,
28 × 19⅝"
Coll. Mattioli, Milan

days — in a Fascist country which had by now become involved in the war. But Manzù, the director of the gallery and Cesare Brandi (who wrote the preface to the catalogue) had the required courage. As was to be expected, the event released a storm of indignation. The Fascist newspaper S t a m p a branded the artist as an enemy of the regime and an 'International Jew'. In addition to this a friend of Manzù's, closely connected with the Vatican, told him that he was threatened with excommunication. This seems all the more strange as the Death of Christ is represented with such devout compassion that there can be no suggestion of rebellion against the Church. On the other hand the political allusions leave no doubt that Christ appears as a victim of Fascism as well. It seems peculiar that the Vatican considered severe punishment for this kind of artistic commentary, while the heads of the aggressor states escaped excommunication. Whereas the exhibition threatened to bring Manzù into conflict with the Church and the government, the Communist underground movement considered him one of their own. He protested against this, however, declaring that he was not so much pro-Communist as anti-Fascist and anti-Nazi.

MEETING WITH FRANCESCA

Before the memorable exhibition in Milan opened, a Baroness Blanc had commissioned the artist to come to Rome and do a portrait of her daughter Francesca. This occurrence became one of the most important events for Manzù during the dark years of the war. When the mother introduced him to the thirteen-year-old child, Manzù not only declared himself ready to make the desired likeness but also expressed the wish to do a life-size nude of the young girl, to which both mother and daughter agreed. In 1940 he spent a whole month in Rome, working busily on a standing nude dancer (which was to become the first of a new series) and on a large figure of Francesca sitting; at the same time he completed a series of drawings.

Young people, and even children, had already appeared quite frequently in Manzù's work, for instance in his 'David' and the 'Girl on a Chair'. In Francesca the artist found precisely the type of which he had dreamed. His preference for youthful bodies arose from a search for specific forms which he wanted to analyze in his work. The flexible, high-bosomed maidens of Cranach or the voluptuous women of Rubens, the strong, full-breasted models of Maillol standing on heavy, pillar-like legs or the slender girls of Manzù, all these are not only expressions of a personal sensual tendency, they also represent the ideal form of a period as recorded in the artist's predilection for certain aesthetic elements selected from among all the phenomena observed in nature. Manzù himself has said that he looked on Francesca as a still-life.

When an artist draws, it is of course mainly the eyes which delight in the beauty of the body that is offered to him, but when he models a figure, his hands, so to speak, take possession of it. In contrast to the sculptor working in stone, chipping out shapes with his chisel, the one who kneads with clay creates forms directly from the moist material. It can hardly be denied that sensual pleasure is part of the work as his hands simultaneously fashion and caress the emerging figure. While the eyes are fixed on the model, the fingers constantly glide over a rendering of its body. In probably no other process of creation is there such an intimate connection between perception and direct sensory expression.

Manzù's apparent preference for delicate and harmonious forms could have exposed him to the danger of 'elegant' works in which the splendid proportions of a figure might have become a self-sufficient purpose. But Manzù stresses specifically that elegance has never played a role in his concepts. In any case he escapes this danger by avoiding professional models and more or less perfect bodies, using instead, as in the case of Francesca, girls whose as yet not completely developed forms correspond less closely to the conventional norms of beauty. There a still clumsy grace and a charming modesty of nudeness prevails; the child is still unconscious of the beauty and seductiveness of her own body. But the artist senses that this ingenuousness will not last much longer and that the bud will soon burgeon into flower. In the works inspired by Francesca, Manzù knew how to capture this unique moment with great tenderness yet without any senti-mentality.

The crouching Francesca, although not really a sculpture in the round, inasmuch as the back remains open and thus brings to mind a very high relief, is a masterpiece of com-position. The completely relaxed pose in which, as is often the case with Manzù, the body appears as a compact mass — with carefully modelled details interrupting the great planes — is itself symbolically expressive of a gradual awakening. The noble, rounded line of the back is balanced and crowned by the head, which is at the same time, via the arms, anchored between the knees, so that despite the contrast of curves and diagonals an appearance of endless rest is achieved. The eye is irresistibly drawn from the bent head, from the narrow shoulders, from the arms — between which the small breasts are nestling — down to the delicate hand which hangs freely between the knees as if left to itself, its fine articulation contrasting with the slender forms of the legs. This hand, fitting into a space created for it, gently breaks open the closed unity of the crouching body and contains an exceptional charm. It represents the 'discovery' of an unusually sensitive artist, part of whose originality is that his works often contain details which are so naturally subordinated to the whole that it may escape many how directly, and with what incredible instinct for plastic form, they have been conceived.

None of the many sketches of Francesca done at the same period were drawn for specific projects since Manzù, when sketching, always prefers to devote himself to purely graphic problems. Nevertheless these drawings, which study the body of the young girl from many angles and in numerous poses, stood him in good stead later. In Manzù's own words, Francesca inspired him so vividly for the next five years (until he met Signora Lampugnani in 1946) that all his nudes of that period contain echoes of her.

GRAND PRIX AT THE QUADRENALE IN ROME, 1942

At the Quadrenale of Rome in 1942 the bronze of Francesca caused great excitement, and the artist was awarded the Grand Prix of the exhibition. In the meantime Manzù continued teaching at Turin until the town was heavily bombarded at the end of that year. He thereupon withdrew, with his wife and three year-old son Pio, to Clusone in the upper valley of Bergamo and established a studio there. In 1943 he was recalled to his post at the Brera and thereafter travelled once a week from Clusone to Milan.

Meanwhile the Allies had landed in Africa, crossed to Sicily and captured Anzio. Although these events clearly indicated the impending defeat of Fascism, those directly concerned did not realize this certainty, and with every new report from the front they felt fear, distress, despair and hope. Nobody knew whether he would survive to the end of the war. In Italy, Austria and Germany the enemies of Hitler and Mussolini were also in the unenviable position of having to wish for the defeat of their own country in order to be free once more.

Under these circumstances further reliefs of the Crucifixion series were created at Clusone. At the same time Manzù returned, with a large relief, to the theme of the artist with his model, which he had already tackled in 1937. He also worked on a free-standing group of a sitting man — a suggested self-portrait — holding a nude woman in his lap. In 1944 he created a number of smaller statues and clay sketches, as if the disturbed times did not permit the artist to concentrate on a large project. He was indeed requested by the Germans to leave his studio, whereupon he deposited his work in a private house and escaped at night, to remain hidden with friends in Bergamo until the end of the war. Francesca visited him there at the suggestion of her mother, but did not pose for him. Meanwhile the Brera Academy had become virtually depopulated. Marini had fled to Switzerland, the painter Carpi had been deported as a Jew and the Fascist Messina had preferred to bolt. When the Americans finally entered Milan in the spring of 1945, they were met at the Brera only by the director, Dr Fernanda Wittgens, and by Manzù.

The post-war period was difficult and unsettled at first, but Manzù could at least return to his own work without, however, giving up his teaching at the Academy. He moved back to Milan where he soon met a young woman, who — exactly as Francesca had done previously — kept him under her spell for some time.

SIGNORA LAMPUGNANI

In 1946 Signora Alice Lampugnani asked the Milan professor of art history, Pacchioni, to recommend a sculptor whom she could commission to do a portrait bust of one of her children. Manzù, to whom she was introduced, was so impressed by her appearance that he asked to be permitted to do a portrait of her. Although he did make a few sketches of the child his main preoccupation for the next two years was a large sculpture of Signora Lampugnani.

The young woman, then in her early thirties, was distinguished not only by her charm but also by her unusual intelligence. She sat for the artist in her own home and was depicted by him in a long dressing-gown which clung closely to her slender body. Whereas Manzù was in the habit of continuing his work in the studio even in the absence of a model, he worked on this new sculpture exclusively in the presence of his sitter, who always found time for him. Over ninety large drawings were thus created simultaneously with the sculpture; in their animated lines and almost passionate directness they belong among Manzù's most beautiful creations. He also worked on a head of the young woman and on two busts, a sign of how greatly the artist was captivated by this encounter.

The creative urge of an artist is probably always released by some event which causes him to tackle a certain problem at a certain time. What distinguishes the case of Manzù from that of others is not only that many of his ideas ferment for years before they take shape, but also that some more or less accidental occurence can engage him so completely as to keep him fascinated for a long time. This does not mean that he will yield his prerogative of choice — the pose of the model and certain details are carefully arranged by him — but this choice itself loses some of its importance inasmuch as he concentrates so intensively on a new experience that he has eyes for nothing else. Indeed he does not even seem to seek a suitable expression but to submit himself passionately to his impressions.

Manzù had not forgotten the girl sitting on a chair, and still dreamed from time to time of doing a new, large version; nor had the memory of the cardinals in the Vatican grown dim and he hoped to give them shape; but the spell which Francesca had cast over him was suddenly broken and all his thoughts and creativity were fixed on the new figure which fate had so unexpectedly sent him.

If the sitting Francesca had not been a completely 'round' sculpture, the figure of Signora Lampugnani is even less so, for here the back remains completely open as if the statue were chased from a large piece of metal. That is why the work should preferably be seen frontally or a little from the side to which the head is turned.

Half-sitting and half-leaning against an indeterminate background, her limbs loosely outstretched, the young woman seems like a symbol of relaxed dreams. Even more important than the musing expression on the gentle countenance are the magnificent curves which stretch from the head right down to the feet, and which are stressed by the many folds of the garment; beneath these the body is at the same time revealed and concealed. Yet the exceptional charm of the work lies not only in the harmony of the lines but also very largely in the differentiation between the garment and the body of the woman. Without aiming at slavish imitation of texture the artist succeeded in giving a slightly animated surface to the long dressing-gown and its tasselled belt which differs — even if almost imperceptibly — from the bust and the hands or the feet which appear below the folds. He also once more surprises the onlooker with some amazing details, such as the gentle swell of the bosom whose hidden magic is revealed discreetly yet emphatically between the lapels of the carelessly worn gown. The hands again play an important role, at the same time interrupting the line leading from the head to the feet, and reminding one of the body underneath the garment. The brilliant arrangement of the planes and the softness of the modelling which avoids sharp contrasts and the illusion of depth — except for the suggestion of the breasts — again stresses Manzù's preference for reliefs, works in which the distinct opposition between animate and inanimate material is frequently shown.

Ever since Manzù has had his sculptures cast in metal he has limited himself to one cast and has destroyed the original plaster. However, the uniqueness of his works is often relieved by variants, each of which is also limited to one cast. The only exceptions to his rule are the sitting Francesca as well as Signora Lampugnani, of which the plaster remained in the possession of the model. With the artist's permission a second cast of the latter was made for the Museum of Modern Art in New York, before the plaster was finally destroyed. (The plaster model of Francesca has met with the same fate.)

Signora Lampugnani did not exert such a lasting impression on the artist as Francesca, whose image pursued him for several years before being displaced by the woman from Milan. After completing the figure in the dressing-gown Manzù felt 'free' to devote himself to other projects. Perhaps the long and intensive sessions in the Lampugnani household had exhausted the excitement, tension, rapture, tenderness and rage to work which had gripped him on meeting the young woman. In 1947 Manzù finally turned to a large version of the naked girl on a chair, the origin of which lay a full sixteen years back.

'GIRL ON A CHAIR

Although the drawings of the child made in 1931 had already been followed in 1933 by a first life-size study chased in copper, there was an interval of four more years before the artist executed a small version in lead. Now, after a further pause of ten years, he attacked a new life-size figure, once more to be cast in lead, while the chair was intended to be of bronze. In contrast to the crouching Francesca and to Signora Lampugnani, this was to be a completely free-standing sculpture. The naked child sits on a fragile chair,

a memento of Manzù's home, one of those banal objects which acquire sentimental importance in the afterglow of memory. (The artist has never parted with this chair, which appears in many of his works and which hangs, almost like a talisman, on the wall of his present new studio.) Even an observer knowing nothing of the special significance of this chair is captivated by the amazing assurance with which an everday object here becomes a true component of a work of art.

The posture of the little girl is completely natural and relaxed, the knees are slightly parted and the hands rest nonchalantly on the thighs. The important thing is that the parallels of the legs and feet are not repeated by the hands, and that there are differentiations in the positions of the arms. In a composition in which the four almost vertical lines of the chair are echoed by the upright posture of the body this artifice was essential to avoid the impression of rigidity; for the same reason a slight diagonal was chosen for the position of the legs.

The nude is very carefully and smoothly executed and every detail is lovingly observed, as for instance the way in which the edge of the chair cuts into the flesh of the thighs. The impression of naturalness is heightened by the chair, which is so faithfully reproduced that it might almost have been cast from the original. It is hard to imagine that this work was created with the help of a handful of old sketches and without the further aid of a model.

The contrast between the young body and the spindly-legged chair is all the more astonishing as both these elements simultaneously form a harmonic unity. This time Manzù has not — as so often before — gathered his model into a compact mass but has, on the contrary, 'opened' the forms so that interstices are created everywhere through which the light can flow and the eye can wander. These interstices are vitally important to the overall impression of the work. The relationship of all parts to each other, the distance between the legs of the girl and the chair, between the shoulders and the hands, between the thighs and the feet, all create a most unusual interplay of mass and space, of volume and surroundings.

The penetrating observation of nature accompanied by a desire for simplification, as well as the indefinable mixture of sensuality and grace, conceal the great boldness which is required to break new trails without employing new methods. In this way the artist managed to provide contemporaneity with an expression of timelessness. Apart from Degas' famous fourteen-year-old dancer with the real muslin tutu there is probably no work of modern sculpture which is so unusual, and yet appears so natural, as Manzù's 'Girl on a Chair'. The great assurance with which they depart from anything created previously is common to both works, but their inventiveness has not become an end in itself. On the contrary, there is no experimentation with surprising elements — as is so often the case with modern sculpture — for the originality is here inseparable from the concept of the work.

After the figure had been completed (it is now in the Museum of Modern Art, Turin), the artist noticed what he usually calls 'possibilities for improvement or slight modifications'. In 1949 he therefore created a new version which he regarded as final; it is also life-size, but this time cast completely in bronze (Mattioli collection, Milan). Its finality, however, did not prevent Manzù from preparing another variant in the same year (Museum of Modern Art, Madrid). After a further interval of six years, another version was created in 1955 (National Museum, Toronto) with three variants (the last of which was miscast). The two others are in the Oslo Museum and the collection of Joseph Hirshhorn, New York. The differences between the seven examples, made between 1947 and 1955, are often slight and yet quite noticeable. In one version, for instance, the girl sits more stiffly and upright in the chair; in other cases the facial expression differs greatly, the cheeks are rounder and the eyes completely cast down. Sometimes the head is changed so much that the girl seems a different child altogether.

The year 1947 also saw the creation of a naked boy with a duck, the two forming a closely connected and very dynamic group. The boy resembles the earlier figure of 'David', who seems to be lying on his back in this case. For the artist himself the most important event of the year was his great one-man show at the Palazzo Reale in Milan, which opened the series of splendid exhibitions held there since that time. The preface to the catalogue was written by Lionello Venturi, recently returned from exile in America, whom the artist had met in Paris before the war.

GRAND PRIX FOR ITALIAN SCULPTURE
AT THE XXIVTH BIENNALE IN VENICE, 1948

The artist's fame had grown steadily since his first exhibition in Rome in 1937, and especially since the Quadrenale of 1942, but this important post-war exhibition confirmed it conclusively. Up to that time his fame had been mainly confined to Italy. In the following year, however, the artist received a room to himself at the Biennale in Venice (further rooms went to Carrà, Marini and Morandi) where he showed, among other things, the 'Girl on a Chair' of 1947. For the first time the international public began to take notice of him, not least because he won the great medal for Italian sculpture; Morandi received the one for painting (at that time Morandi was nearly sixty, while Manzù was barely forty).

For an ageing master success is often a kind of 'compensation' which follows long years of neglect, thus throwing a glimmer of fame on the evening of his life; but for a man at the height of his powers success not only brings satisfaction, it acts as an incentive; indeed, he has continually to prove himself worthy of it, almost to compete with himself. It is therefore not surprising that Manzù was particularly active in the years following 1948, and that he took several projects in hand more or less simultaneously. At first a small, seated cardinal brought the planned series closer. Then he participated in the international competition for a portal of St Peter's in Rome, for which he received the commission in 1950. From then on he turned from time to time to studies for this portal, which was to commemorate the 'Triumph of Saints and Martyrs of the Teaching and Professing Church'. It is characteristic, however, that his first designs, accepted by the Vatican, underwent such radical changes with the passage of time that they bear hardly any relation to the final version created sixteen years later, of which even the basic theme had been changed completely.

In any case the artist concerned himself further with the problems of relief, which were of particular consequence to this new commission. At about this time he also made some high reliefs of almost free-standing figures against a uniform background. It does not seem impossible that memories of the curiously animated twelfth-century bronze doors of San Zeno Maggiore — which he had admired during his military service in Verona — guided him in this new direction. Of prime importance is that he revealed, in the grouping of figures which are almost free from the background, a brilliant sense of composition and of spatial distribution. Manzù not only displayed in the modelling a complete mastery of his craft but achieved, as he had done with a 'Crucifixion' and a 'Deposition' of 1951, an exceptionally penetrating and rhythmic representation of grief; each figure is distinguished by a great tenderness, while forming at the same time a part of

54

PORTRAIT OF A LADY, 1946
Black chalk, 24⅜ × 18⅞"
Coll. Lampugnani, Milan

the whole. The place allocated to each figure, its isolation, the distance or proximity to a neighbour, all add to its dramatic beauty. The conjunction of deep empathy and the most delicate execution gave magnificent results. It is not without importance that Manzù's renewed preoccupation with reliefs led to a renewed involvement with religious themes.

A large 'Susanna' was also created at this time, the artist working from 1949 to 1954 on the clothed, stretched-out young woman with bare legs, while a related reclining figure occupied him even from 1942 to 1953. Like Signora Lampugnani, 'Susanna' is distinguished by the splendid arrangement of the clothes in contrast to the smooth representation of the body. A naked thigh and a raised knee most forcefully accentuate the predominating horizontals.

THE SERIES OF CARDINALS

Whereas Manzù had required ten years — from 1943 to 1953 — to create a small, seated cardinal, he now attacked this old project with vigour. The first drawing of the subject dated from 1934, the first sculpture from 1938. Between 1949 and 1950 the first large cardinal was created, and this was followed one after another by many more, sitting and standing, small, large, and even more than life-size; over fifty of them altogether, of which the last was completed exactly ten years later.

Manzù's success had improved his material conditions considerably (without, however, salvaging his shattered marriage), yet he remained faithful to certain original emotions connected with his home and his childhood. The subjects for reliefs derived from the New Testament perpetuated the devout faith of his mother, which he himself had since outgrown; the chair of the sitting girl recalled the house of his father, and the solemn prelates also intermingled impressions of his youth in Bergamo with later ones. When asked, the artist always stresses that the cardinals did not interest him as a typically religious theme but represented for him more the character of still-life (a word that he had applied also to Francesca), so that no deeper significance should be attached to them than to a plate of apples, for example. He even likes to add that he might just as easily have represented matadors. There were, however, no bullfights in Bergamo, whereas the boy often met church dignitaries. Their visual impression became an inspiration for him, a problem of artistic creation which, so to speak, pursued him for years. For a long time the mitred priests enveloped in canonicals had ceased to be connected with his personal religious beliefs; his youthful memories were only concerned with the picturesque garments, curious vestige of a splendour-loving past. Now Manzù proved with his statues that this clothing was not only 'picturesque' but also eminently 'statuesque'.

The artist naturally knows that the vestments of the cardinals are much more baroque in character than he has shown them, and that priests in general do not bear themselves as hieratically as they appear in his statues. He consciously omitted or altered many details, especially since he had to leave out some of the most essential elements of the robes, such as the colour, the jewels and the splendours of the moiré silks. In his own words the important characteristic of these works is 'a general tendency for simplification. As the volumes are great and monumental, I preferred to create them on a life-size scale, or even a little bigger.'

In Manzù's hands the cardinals were transformed into compact forceful volumes, enlivened by extremely tender modelling and generously draped folds. The massiveness of the volumes is stressed by the economy of lines and the simplicity of plastic means, yet the artist avoided the danger of both primitiveness and monotony. In fact the few, decisive lines are not applied to the form from without, but correspond to an inner necessity and are an indissoluble part of the form itself. In his reliefs and in some of his statues Manzù occasionally draws certain lines in the wet clay; they indicate details and serve to animate the material. In the case of the cardinals such lines are used neither for ornamentation nor for the suggestion of details, but only for the organization of largely conceived and homogeneous shapes.

The secret of true sculpture lies in the fact that a volume has to be conceived from within, and this can be done not through expediencies or clever tricks, but through obedience to the law which requires a form to be harmonious, stable and revolving; to be, in a word, developed logically. Only in one respect does Manzù make concessions to simplification: in his cardinals four aspects are stressed — frontal, profiles and back. But the same also applies to Egyptian sculpture.

With Signora Lampugnani the artist had been able to hint at the presence of the body beneath the dressing-gown; with the cardinals the body is completely covered, in some of them even the hands are invisible. All details are subordinated to the almost geometric pyramidal form, which in many cases extends without break from the hem of the robe to the tip of the mitre. Yet the pyramid-like silhouette of these works is not 'forced' upon nature by a whim of the artist. However stylized the vestments may be, they always appear as what they are: an envelope for the body, even if this body itself remains invisible. And when occasionally the hands (or one hand) appear from between the folds, they are never merely an added naturalistic element which interrupts the formal strength of the volumes, but always a part of that invisible body that supports these monumental garments.

A simplification of this kind naturally makes the highest demands on technical skill. Manzù once again showed his astonishing mastery: the large planes are never lifeless, the folds are never rigid; by means of extremely sensitive modelling the surface is made to vibrate. Following the contours of the body, the folds swing sometimes as if sharply etched, sometimes softly rounded, their shadows always regulating the parts exposed to the light. This subtle animation of uniform planes and the amazing freedom of conception earned the artist the respect of many sculptors whose own paths had led them toward abstractions. More than they valued the sensitivity of execution they admired the boldness of invention which, within the framework of fidelity to nature, rids the form of all that is inessential.

Literary explanations add little of value to important sculpture, but it was probably inevitable that these cardinals should invite manifold interpretations. While some saw in them the glorification of the Church and its dignitaries, others thought they discovered in them an anti-clerical attitude. One East German author apologized, so to speak, to his readers, because although 'progressive' he yet loved these cardinals, explaining: 'I see in them the image of the Inquisition, cruel but without might. I see in them a bloodless and yet powerful relationship, frozen in isolation, to the surrounding world . . .'

Manzù vehemently denies having wished to express any feelings such as cruelty or others. He constantly stresses that he had no hidden thoughts when he made this series and that his intention had been neither to attack nor to defend Catholicism. As a matter of fact he consciously avoided giving the cardinals a specific expression or the features of a living prototype; for him they represented, as he says, 'not the majesty of the church, but the majesty of form'.

The cardinals were all conceived without a model, and their faces were freely invented by the artist. The single exception is the seated Cardinal Giacomo Lercaro completed in 1953. An admirer of this prince of the Church commissioned this work and the Bolognese

CARDINAL, 1940
Pen and ink, 15¼ × 10⅜"
Coll. Prof. Umberto Vittorir
Milan

prelate willingly sat for a few studies. The statue, more than eight feet high, now stands in a rather dark corner of the Basilica of San Petronio in Bologna. It is the only example of this series which, as the actual portrait of a priest, has a true connection with religion.

Around that time the artist was introduced to another cardinal by Monsignor Giuseppe De Luca, but did not then make a portrait of him. Monsignor De Luca was a priest in Rome who stood close to the Vatican although he did not despise the pleasures of life nor hide his liberal attitude. As a friend of Croce and many other Italian authors — some of them even of the Left — he was highly respected for his wide knowledge and his unprejudiced interest in cultural questions. Manzù had met this unusual man some years after the war, and frequently and happily discussed the most diverse problems with him. The prelate encouraged the artist in moments of depression, especially while Manzù tackled the gigantic portal of St Peter's, and gave him the necessary self-confidence for the execution of this commission. In the middle 'fifties De Luca introduced Manzù to Angelo Roncalli, the Patriarch of Venice. The artist was deeply touched that the cardinal, who had been born in Bergamo in 1881, clearly remembered his father, the poor cobbler and sexton.

Besides the intensive activity with the cardinals and some new projects — among them the first studies for a new series which Manzù calls 'Dance Steps' and which deal mostly with the standing nude of a female dancer — the 'fifties brought other, portentous events. His marriage finally broke up completely after nearly twenty years. His wife left him and Pio, their only surviving child, born in 1939. In 1952 Manzù obtained a legal separation, there being no possibility of divorce according to Italian law.

During those years Francesca suddenly reappeared. She had married a famous nobleman while still very young, but no longer lived with him. The artist made a number of drawings of her which he exhibited as a series in Turin, but which he destroyed afterwards, except for a few which he had already 'lightheartedly' given away. He saw Francesca from time to time, but her beautiful features bore increasing signs of a tempestuous and unbridled existence. One day she threw herself from a window and, on the pavement, found the death she sought.

In the spring of 1953 Manzù's first one-man show outside Italy opened at the Hanover Gallery, directed by Erica Brausen, in London. Since the end of the war the artist's works had been included in many group exhibitions of contemporary art — not only in Paris and London, but also Munich, Hamburg, Rotterdam, Brussels and Antwerp, in Athens and Madrid, in Philadelphia, Chicago, São Paulo and many other cities — but this was the first comprehensive show of his works abroad. The event seemed important enough for him to travel to England, the first time he left Italy since 1936. In London he visited the many public collections and was particularly enthralled by the Elgin Marbles in the British Museum.

During all these years Manzù, despite his great productivity, had continued teaching at the Brera. He considered it a moral duty to place his experience at the disposal of the students in his care, and to instil in them not only his love of art but also his knowledge of the handicraft of sculpture. After ten years of teaching at the school, however, he was 'discouraged and disappointed' by the academic methods because he had 'never succeeded in transforming this institution into a living organism'. He was indignant that so many professors should subordinate their teaching to their personal interests, their vanity, their weaknesses or simply to their indifference, and that so many painters or sculptors who had failed as artists should take employment at the academy as an expediency. Manzù therefore decided to expound his ideas about a radical reform in the teaching of art in a memorandum to the responsible Ministry. The minister was duly impressed by these suggestions and did what ministers always do in such circumstances: he appointed a commission. Since this commission was composed of exactly those academic professors whom Manzù considered unfit for their jobs, it came to the not surprising conclusion that there was absolutely no necessity to change the existing order of things, and even less to abolish the academies and replace them with international schools of art, as Manzù had suggested. Thereupon Manzù left the Brera in 1954.

APPOINTMENT TO THE INTERNATIONAL SUMMER ACADEMY AT SALZBURG — MEETING WITH INGE

By coincidence, Friedrich Welz invited the artist to come to the International Summer Academy in Salzburg in the same year that he gave up, not without regret, his teaching post at the Brera. Kokoschka was already directing his 'School of Seeing' which had been inaugurated in 1953 and Manzù, for his part, took over the entirely independent class of sculpture. He spent several weeks in Salzburg where he found himself surrounded by a crowd of industrious students from many countries. Despite an assistant interpreting to the best of his ability, Manzù could not easily exchange ideas with them but was able to transmit his opinions by correcting their efforts and demonstrating his conceptions through direct intervention. Because he himself could not work in the presence of the students, he was given a small room adjoining the large classroom studio. He used it rarely, however, since he always held himself at the disposal of the class, tirelessly going from one to the other to watch over their progress.

One day, when there was no model, Welz applied to the local dancing school and found a young girl from Munich willing to act as a substitute. But she was not prepared to pose in the nude and insisted on wearing her leotard. The sight of this young dancer, named Inge, was as exciting and disconcerting to Manzù as had been his previous encounters with Francesca and Signora Lampugnani. He again found himself in the presence of someone who embodied precisely that which he wished to shape and express. Although he had been concerned for several years with the theme of 'Dance Steps', he had at first merely created upright nudes, followed shortly afterwards by dancers standing on their points. In Inge he now discovered, in his own words, 'limitless possibilities' for this project. He soon began to work in the isolation of his small private studio on a 'Dancer' after Inge and persuaded her to remain his model when the Summer Academy had finished.

At that time Inge was not yet twenty and wanted to train as a professional dancer. She must have been deeply affected by the intensity of the artist and the unexpected role that fate had thrust upon her. While Manzù drew and modelled her tirelessly, and while her face and body were recreated in one work after another, she understood it to be her duty to yield to this eruption of creative passion. She did so with the greatest modesty and patience; a kind of humble sacrifice to the artist and his work. Neither tall nor of the fragile elegance that characterizes so many dancers, Inge combined radiant health with the particular grace that the study of classical dancing lends to all bodies. Her comparatively wide shoulders and powerful thighs were more plastically moulded than the lean figures of most ballerinas which consist only of muscles and sinews. But it was the noble beauty of her regular features which especially attracted Manzù; the fine straight nose, the

INGE, 1956
Pencil, 15¾ × 19⅝"
Private Collection

VEGETABLE STILL-LIFE, 1957
Pen and ink with wash,
$11\frac{3}{8} \times 16\frac{1}{8}$"
Galerie Welz, Salzburg

almond-shaped eyes, the conspiciously delineated mouth, and the full lips which showed some peculiar vertical lines rather like small cracks or splits; they appear in nearly all the countless busts and drawings which the artist has made since then. Inge has subsequently dominated Manzù's work almost completely, more strongly than any of his previous encounters.

Despite his preoccupation with Inge, the artist at first continued to work on some of his earlier series, the cardinals and also the girl sitting on a chair, of which the last version with variants was executed in 1955. In the summer of that year he taught at Salzburg once again, where he met Inge's younger sister Sonja — at that time only a child — of whom he modelled a very delicate portrait. He soon represented her in various youthful poses, especially as an ice-skater in a short, flared skirt.

Friedrich Welz, who was at that time organizing a travelling exhibition of Manzù's works in Austria and Germany, succeeded in interesting the artist in a project for a portal of the Salzburg Cathedral. Although Manzù should have devoted himself to the already-commissioned portal for St Peter's, he busied himself with this new plan and created some designs, considering this commission as a kind of preparation for the much more extensive task that awaited him in Rome.

At the 1956 Biennale in Venice Manzù was represented by a number of important works; in a special room a group of large cardinals was assembled in a kind of solemn 'council'. Although these bronzes were not conceived with the intention of being seen together, their confrontation created a most impressive whole. It also showed how extensively the individual figures varied from one another and the great ingenuity which gave each statue its individual stamp within the framework of a continually repeated overall shape, this individuality being achieved by details of posture, hands, folds, etc. The artist himself considers this the best of his many exhibitions. (It aroused in the author of these lines the desire to meet the sculptor, a wish that was fulfilled during the next year.)

In 1956 Manzù continued his preparations for the Salzburg portal and also created a number of studies on the theme of 'motherhood'. Besides this, Inge inspired new busts and figures of dancers. The fact that the artist was again active in the Salzburg Summer Academy probably entailed a further interest in the problem of art instruction, now considered from a less locally conditioned viewpoint. This question was close to Manzù's heart in spite or perhaps even because of his failure in 1954. The following year he conceived a detailed project which he sent, not to the Ministry this time, but to the Town Council of Milan.

This document, dated March 1957, proposed the creation of an international school, a kind of laboratory of art, to be built with the help of the Milan city government. Manzù pointed out that he considered it essential that 'young people treading the thorny path of art must have the opportunity not only to develop their artistic and mental faculties in order to reach their goal, but must simultaneously be supplied with a knowledge of handicraft, all the more so as manual ability and familiarity with technical questions are not external or trivial factors but the inner and decisive basis for the shaping of a work.'

Manzù's suggestions were greeted with great acclaim, especially among young Italian architects and also abroad. Various Milanese art patrons promised considerable sums of money for the foundation of the school, others pledged support, the Town Council accepted the project, and the result was . . . nothing. For the second time the bold plans of the artist foundered on the passive resistance of bureaucrats.

Manzù was deeply disappointed and to this day speaks of his failure with great bitterness. But he could at least, for a few weeks each year, instruct his pupils in Salzburg along his guiding lines; these he clearly expressed in a speech he made at the end of one of his summer courses:

'I am happy after all to have sacrificed a month of my work for you. I am neither a professor nor a master, but simply a sculptor who has the same aims you have. If I have any advantage over you it is solely the fact that I have thirty-five years of work behind me. I transmit what I can to you because I want to pass on what I too have received from others. The ideal school should be a companionship between teacher and pupils where problems are posed so that they can be solved together. That, I believe, is how tuition should be.

'I only wanted to advise you about the possibilities of technical solutions, and to show you the way, namely, the efforts required to formulate your ideas. You must be willing to receive help, for I myself would go to the ends of the earth if I knew I would gain some new understanding. If I could improve that which I create by only one degree, I would be prepared to give my life for it. That is the only way to achieve something. If any one among you does not feel the same way, I would advise him to give up sculpture at once and to start something else, for he will never attain a personal inspiration, artistic form and artistic expression.

'Work with love! I never neglect my work because I know what efforts a sculpture will cost me, and my devotion to a work is so great that I lovingly follow it to the end, like a mother. Pursue your work in all its phases — armature, clay, plaster, wax, bronze, etc. — with a love that does not permit any stage of your work to be done by others . . .

'Do not be afraid of nature — she will not hinder you! If you work with nature, even reproduce her, you can create something new, for the result will not be something external but that which lies hidden in yourselves . . .

'It is essential to subordinate all talent to the artistic urge, to sacrifice everything for it; only thus can one reach true artistry. Leopardi said: "You cannot reach paradise in a carriage." The sacrifice is necessary if one truly wishes to possess nature. Even the abstract is inspired by nature. Klee and Kandinsky had nature before their eyes. All artists, even the Egyptians, the Greeks, the Byzantines and those of the Renaissance and the Baroque, started from nature. But your work remains the most important factor; however, work only if you are gripped by an inner, spiritual excitement. If you do not feel this inner excitement, it is senseless to continue working since this means that you have nothing to say. A work of art springs only from an attitude to love and creation. Do not imagine that you can build a world of forms from preconceived plastic ideas that are not your own. Try to follow nature, and follow her freely! The solution of her problems comes through work. A genius is not born — but only grows to be one. If it were possible to work twenty-four hours a day, I would advise you to do so.

'The passions which move me and each of you must never be allowed to dominate our care for our work; this care must always come first. Only through complete devotion can one achieve something. The equilibrium between the work of art and the artist consists in the fact that human passions never gain ascendancy over the spiritual.

'The true essential of your work is that an inner fire must grip the material, which should no longer remain a material, because the substance that comes under our hands must be spiritualized. The hardest stone worked by the Egyptians no longer shows any trace of the hardness and difficulty of the material. The plastic concept must not be inspired by formal prejudices but only by your love. This I say not only to you, but to myself as well.'

However deeply felt and correctly conceived these opinions may be it cannot be denied that no teaching, not even the most brilliant, can awaken talents that are not already present in embryo. In this sense a teacher is above all a gardener whose solicitous care helps tender plants to develop fully. Manzù is all the more conscious of this, as his unconditional devotion to his vocation naturally makes him demanding, so that he has little patience or tolerance for botched work or for those who regard art chiefly as a pleasant way to pass the time. Like every teacher, he hoped that among the many pupils who came to him in Salzburg from Germany, Austria, Holland, England, Italy and even America, there would be some latent talents which would ripen under his guidance. Beyond this, his teaching activity gave him pleasant human contacts, forced him to come a little out of his shell and helped him to formulate his own views more sharply. Convictions alone are not enough; to transmit one's ideas to others, clearly conceived lines of thought are essential.

When I came to know Manzù in Milan in the autumn of 1957 he maintained that he had given up teaching as he no longer 'believed' in it, but that he might consider advising a few pupils in his craft. Despite this he continued, for a few years, to teach at the Salzburg Summer Academy, and has until now not taken any private students into his studio.

The artist was then almost fifty years old, a compact man of modest mien and calm bearing, but who became animated when the conversation touched upon questions of importance to him. His hair had begun to recede from his forehead, and he always wore a cap or a straw hat (sometimes even in winter) in his studio and occasionally at home. His features did not seem particularly impressive; they are dominated by a long nose, slightly grooved at the tip. He did not look like an 'artist' and could easily have been taken for an artisan or business man. But he could never have been mistaken for a dull mind, for the expression of his eyes — which observe everything sharply — is extremely lively and even shrewd. One is indeed quickly convinced of his great intelligence; his friendliness and sense of humour are clearly evident. But, as with many shy and nervous people, his moods can change very suddenly, all the more so as he gets excited easily and then, like so many Italians, does not always control himself.

He had established a frugal and not too spacious but well-lit studio on the ground floor of an unpretentious house in Milan. A number of large plaster figures stood around haphazardly, many of them 'Dancers' inspired by Inge. He mentioned that this subject had occupied him before he met Inge, but that it was she who had enabled him to explore fully all the possibilities that lay in the figure of a nude dancer. Now he intended to turn to a new series which harked back directly to Inge — and partially to her small sister Sonja — namely the figure of an ice-skater. (At that time Manzù again began to devote himself to painting; he was mainly occupied with the group of a 'Painter and his Model' which he also treated in reliefs and free-standing sculptures, but he did not show any of these works.)

In his home there were countless drawings for the reliefs of the portals of the Vatican and the Salzburg Cathedral, the latter having been definitely commissioned in March 1957. For every one of the rectangular compositions there were many studies which suggested the most diverse solutions, each dealing exquisitely with the problems of spatial arrangements. Some of these drawings seemed most carefully executed, others were rapidly done. The artist was so obsessed by the project that he put down his ideas anywhere; among the sketches were some on paper napkins or any other material that came to hand. In many of the feminine figures it was easy to recognize the classical beauty of Inge, who now represented Manzù's ideal type of woman. Besides, he also devoted himself to nature studies, especially animals. It was difficult to imagine how he would be able to select a limited number of compositions for the two portals from this mass of drawings fermenting with ideas, although on leafing through the sketches the artist himself sometimes indicated projects which he had discarded in the meanwhile. (He had, for instance, given up the representation of Salome with the head of John the Baptist, intended for the Vatican, and chosen instead the scene of the actual beheading.) Manzù was clearly in the process of selecting, from among the surfeit of ideas which had been haphazardly jotted down on paper, those elements best fitted to his purpose.

THE PORTAL OF SALZBURG CATHEDRAL

The main Salzburg portal was to glorify 'Love' in the form of 'Charity', while the neighbouring portals, on the themes of 'Faith' and 'Hope', were commissioned from other sculptors. The artist was advised that the virtue of love was to be represented by saints noted for their charitable deeds and who also had close connections with the archdiocese of Salzburg. Apart from four reliefs concerned with the benevolence or martyrdom of these saints, Manzù created door-handles in the shape of ears of corn and grape-vines — eucharistic symbols — and a lower frieze of four birds symbolically pertaining to charity: a brooding hen, a raven, a dove and a pelican. Each door of the portal is about fifteen feet high and more than three feet wide. On the inner side appear two free-standing cardinals, the founders of the archbishopric; they are mounted on little bases, are gilded and serve as door-handles. Above them are fields of intertwined olive branches in a style somewhat reminiscent of art nouveau. The same pair of cardinals can also be found on the key of the portal for which, as for all other details, there are a number of preliminary studies.

The rich tradition in Italy not only of relief but especially of bronze portals — from the romanesque representations of San Zeno in Verona to the famous compositions of Ghiberti for the doors of the baptistry in Florence — gave the artist the opportunity to be guided in his project by the splendid archievements of numerous predecessors. But Manzù did not lean on the accomplishments of the past, particularly because his efforts to simplify prevented him from deriving any inspiration from Ghiberti's highly complicated compositions in which several events and numerous figures are combined in a small space. He was much more enthusiastic about Egyptian low reliefs which seem 'drawn' on the stone, although he knew them mainly from reproductions. Moreover he also admired Donatello and the reliefs of Amadeo in the Capella Colleoni in Bergamo, which he had known since childhood (early memories appear time and again in his work). An exhibition of Giovanni Pisano — who initiated the Gothic and foreshadowed the Renaissance — which Manzù saw in Pisa in 1948 also left a lasting impression. Pisano often reduced gestures to essentials and freed his forms of all trivialities, even when they were covered by richly draped garments.

When it came to filling the large areas of the Salzburg doors, Manzù remained faithful to his credo, which he likes to summarize in the following words: 'My method of work always depends on me alone, on that which I can do.' What he could do, above all, was to draw on paper with fluid lines, exquisite curves, form-giving shadows; on wet clay with equally fluid lines, exquisite curves and form-giving modelling. Indeed, for him a low relief is just as natural, basic and direct a form of expression as a drawing (as he sometimes draws from models, so he occasionally works on a relief with the aid of drawings). Both these

70

SAINT SEVERIN AS PROTECTOR OF WOMEN, 1958. Study for the Portal of Salzburg Cathedral Red pen and wash, 25¼ × 19¼" Albertina, Vienna

types of Manzù's work are inseparable. In general, relief could perhaps be regarded as a stage between drawing and sculpture in the round, had not Manzù found in relief a technique so completely befitting his creative will that it became an independent and essential part of his work.

For Manzù, therefore, reliefs are not merely occasional works but a specific form of expression for his thoughts and feelings. They give him the chance to solve in a plastic language certain problems which interest him from a point of view of draughtmanship and composition. He is probably the only contemporary sculptor to whom this applies, which is doubtless why he was selected for the work in Salzburg and Rome. There was no danger of his succumbing to the 'artiness' which lurks behind so much modern religious art, and from which the creators of the other two portals in Salzburg are not completely free. Right from the start Manzù did not conceive his portal simply as a surface to be animated but as a surface to be creatively formed; even the obligatory anecdotal nature of the church legends had to take second place to his demand for an overall harmony.

More important than the representation of the individual saints and their virtues is the style in which the doors are divided into fields, long on top and almost square below, with empty areas in between where traces of casting accidentals have been left. The equilibrium, which might have been upset by this stressing of the upper half, is re-established by four birds at the base; they are worked in high relief and their strong shadows give the necessary accent to the lower edge of the doors. A particularly important, though hardly noticed, detail is the occasional breaking of the rectangular compositions of the reliefs: a foot here and a lance there cut across the sharply scratched frame, thus avoiding the impression of too much rigidity. In this way the reliefs are organically bound to the ground area of the portal.

The treatment of the reiligious themes shows how extensively Manzù was guided by purely artistic considerations. St Notburga of Rattenberg, a pious maid of the thirteenth century, is regarded as the patron saint of agriculture in the alpine regions of Salzburg. Her symbols, accordingly, are usually a sickle, a milking pail, a bunch of keys, bread or a sheaf of corn. Manzù simply lets her hold only a few ears of corn. On the other hand it is known that the Blessed Engelbert Kolland, born in the Ziller valley, was killed by a Turk during a rebellion against the Christians in 1860 while serving as a missionary in Damascus. Manzù gave particular poignancy to his death by showing it as a beheading, which is by no means historically certain. (It is true that the theme of a martyr kneeling diagonally with the opposing figure of the headsman almost at right angles and the head floating freely in the air had interested him strongly in connection with the death of John the Baptist; he had devoted a large number of drawings and preliminary studies to this subject.) The fact that the visibly affected St Notburga witnesses this cruel event, although her death antedated that of the Blessed Engelbert Kolland by seven centuries, indicates the poetic license with which the artist treated the designated material. Manzù similarly chose a little-known episode for his representation of St Francis of Assisi. In fact the artist had a completely free hand in his choice of treatment of the various themes once the saints to be honoured had been selected.

In the Salzburg portal Manzù was concerned with creating four independent relief compositions for which the saints were merely a pretext. Yet he was conscious of the fact that, despite the variations of proportions, he had to find a general rhythm in order to unify the reliefs into a balanced whole. He succeeded in this largely by the treatment of the surface which, as in nearly all his works, depends on unusually sensual modelling where soft contours and decisive lines — surrounded by light and shade — are unified to

77

create astonishingly subtle, yet always clear, forms and relationships. At the same time the purpose of the commission was never forgotten for, despite the monumental scale, the expression of the figures is one of deeply moving mysticism, which can hardly escape even those not familiar with the various events and their religions significance.

The Salzburg portal was completed in 1958 and solemnly inaugurated on 28 July. Simultaneously Friedrich Welz arranged an exhibition of the manifold studies and sketches for it. While engrossed in this work Manzù had sometimes found relaxation in other projects; he busied himself particularly with a new series, 'Artist and Model', in which — in a manner sometimes reminiscent of Picasso etchings — a standing nude (Inge) confronts a sitting or crouching, bearded painter. This subject, in which spatial relationships play a predominant role, as in so many of Manzù's compositions, was treated in a number of oil paintings too. He also made further portraits of Inge and her sister Sonja, who can be recognized in a life-size ice-skater. Finally he created his last cardinals.

In the same year Manzù prepared a four-and-a-half foot high new design for the portal of St Peter's. It diverged strongly from previous projects and more closely resembled the formula chosen for Salzburg. This confirms that the Salzburg undertaking was really a preliminary step for the commission from the Vatican. Martyrs of the church were again the focal point of this plan, which once more included a beheading with the severed head floating in space; this time it was the biblically recorded death of John the Baptist. (However, in the final version of the doors, this composition, with which the artist had wrestled for years, was omitted.) Manzù left Milan in 1958 to start work on the portal in Rome, but Pope Pius XII, during whose primacy a Vatican commission had placed the original order, died before the artist could dedicate himself to the new task.

POPE JOHN XXIII

Pius XII's successor was Angelo Roncalli, the Patriarch of Venice, who came from Bergamo and who mounted the papal throne in his seventy-seventh year. A centuries-old tradition demanded that a portrait bust should be started at once and Pope John remembered the artist son of a sexton from Bergamo, whom he had met some years previously through his friend Monsignor Giuseppe De Luca. So it came about Manzù received the official commission to do a portrait of the new pope, a man who soon gained, even outside Catholic circles, deep respect and admiration as a wise and progressive father of the Church. Monsignor De Luca was sometimes present when the artist was called to the Vatican to sketch the pope, who preferred to sit for his portrait on Sunday mornings when he had some spare time.

Manzù did not find this new project an easy one. For many years he had only done portraits when he himself felt like it; nevertheless he did not hesitate a moment in accepting the honour of such a commission, although it took some time before he felt equal to the task. The tenacity with which he often concentrated on certain themes or human types did not permit a sudden change in his methods. At first the artist thought of portraying the pope in the papal crown, but he soon realized that with his cardinals he had always 'invented' the head in relation to the canonicals, whereas here he had to do the opposite; a life-like portrait had to be created independent of the head-covering.

It cannot be denied that the countenance of John XXIII possessed nothing of the ascetic severity of Pius XII, and that the mildness of his nature was expressed in features of no particular distinction. Even ugliness can have very picturesque or sculptural qualities, whereas attributes of the soul are not necessarily shown by external signs. Wisdom and

78

STUDY FOR A PIETA, 1944
Pen and ink with wash
Coll. Van der Elst, Brussels

goodness, warmth and modesty provide the face with much less interesting lines than, for instance, conceit or cruelty, hatred or treachery. It is not surprising, then, that Manzù modelled, in succession, three busts of the pope before he was even moderately satisfied with the result. At the same time he made relief profiles of John XXIII for two medals, which proved, perhaps more than his busts, that he had in the meanwhile captured the personality of the venerable man.

The friendly, deeply human nature of the pope, who often conversed with him in the homely dialect of Bergamo, made a deep impression on the sculptor. Eventually he plucked up his courage, doubtless aided by De Luca, to confess that he was not particularly happy with the theme for the portal of St Peter's, 'The Triumph of the Saints and Martyrs of the Church', and would prefer to depict the death of the saints and martyrs. John XXIII listened benevolently and not only granted him complete freedom of inspiration, but also permitted him to change the project into a 'Portal of Death' the leitmotiv of which was to be the highest and last moment in the life of every human being. The pope spoke with great clarity and simplicity: he thoroughly understood that the artist had difficulty with the portal and found his dissatisfaction and hesitancy quite comprehensible. Since Manzù wished to represent the theme of death in a new and daring way, he could do so, although this was perhaps unusual in a basilica. In any case he, the pope, had unlimited confidence in him ... Incidentally it was soon discovered that the portal for which the new bronze doors were destined was once called the 'Door of Death'; it had been used almost exclusively for the funerals of important personages.

The sincere understanding which the pope showed towards his problems encouraged Manzù finally to tackle in earnest the project for which the first designs had been created in 1948. Such lengthy delays were not unusual with the artist, but in this case there was the added fact that the task seemed so overwhelming, and the responsibility so oppressive, that he was in two minds whether to relinquish the commission. Since John XXIII had now removed the last obstacles from his path and even urged him in a paternal way to get to work, nothing stood in the way of the realization of the portal.

Yet Manzù still hesitated. Creative men often delay embarking upon great projects, less because they are 'frightened' of them than because they know from the start how demanding such a task will be, and to what degree it will actually take possession of them. They prefer to concern themselves with less exacting work and sometimes even find excuses for delaying the more weighty undertaking. Not only is a clear head needed to concentrate on a great assignment but also the will-power not to be deflected by anything else for a long time, the ability to avoid whatever may prove distracting, and the courage to shut oneself and one's work off from the surrounding world. While he seemingly avoided starting work on the portal of St Peter's, Manzù knew full well that one day he would engross himself unreservedly in this task; it only remained to await the psychological moment.

GREAT TRAVELLING EXHIBITION 1959—60

In 1959 Manzù continued to busy himself without forgetting about the portal. In the summer of that year, Welz organized an important exhibition of his works in Munich. It was subsequently shown in Frankfurt, then in the Nationalgalerie of Berlin and the Ateneum in Helsinki before reaching Salzburg in the summer of 1960, where the artist enriched the show with several additional pieces. Installed in a park with the shadows of the trees playing on them, the great bronzes looked splendid. While teaching once more at the

Salzburg Summer Academy (it was his last appearance there) Manzù began in his small private studio a portrait bust of his friend and colleague Kokoschka. He sketched the painter's head, which has the dignity of a Roman patrician, and his mighty torso in clay and completed the portrait later in Rome.

In the autumn of 1960, the travelling exhibition went from Salzburg to London where it was impressively installed in the Tate Gallery and finally captured the Anglo-American world for the artist. Indeed, he soon received two commissions for fountains from Detroit, and the architect Yamasaki invited him to America. In the autumn of 1961 Manzù travelled to the United States for the first and, up to now, only time.

JOURNEY TO THE UNITED STATES

How vivid and happy are the recollections of this short visit! With the exception of a few days in Detroit, Manzù spent his time mainly in New York. He wanted nothing to escape him. At first, naturally, he was interested in the many art galleries in New York — among them the World House Gallery which up to then had represented him in North America — and in the four most important museums of the city. At the Metropolitan Museum and the Frick Collection he particularly admired the old masters, not least El Greco and Velasquez with whom he was much less familiar than with the Italian masters. The impressionists also continued to attract him; he could study them in the Museum of Modern Art, where he also found a comprehensive collection of contemporary art, practically unrivalled in its completeness (Manzù himself is represented there with the second cast of Signora Lampugnani). Finally he visited the recently opened Guggenheim Museum. He was deeply impressed by the richness and admirable arrangement of these public collections. He was also fascinated by the everyday life of the town: the colourful street scenes, the friendliness of the people, the cool beauty of the women.

With almost childish joy and ceaseless amazement Manzù absorbed the many wonders of the new world: the unbelievable silence of the completely deserted canyons of Wall Street on a Sunday morning; the majestic, almost arrogant skyscrapers of Rockefeller Centre (the Fascist symbols on the Italian building still shamefacedly boarded up); the noise and glaring lights of Broadway; the overwhelming beauty of the city, with its countless windows shining at night; a restaurant on the fiftieth floor (Manzù found express elevators rather eerie); the gay bustle of the youthful bohemians in Greenwich Village; the pitiful display of a sleepy and unappetizing striptease dancer in a dark cellar club; the improbably grotesque performance of the 'Bowery Follies', where old women of seventy or over, richly bedecked in feathers and sequins, either sang abominably or bared their miserable thighs; the ear- and heart-rending jazz trumpeters in Harlem; and many other things.

In Detroit Manzù was deferentially received and introduced to the two architectural sites for which his fountains were destined. After his return to Rome he designed a group for the mighty building of the Detroit Gas Company; a girl stretched out, lying on an small plinth in the middle of the water and a squatting boy playing a flute at a corner of the basin. This model appeared too horizontal to the architect Yamasaki and was abandoned by the artist to be replaced by a more than life-size dancer with raised arms.

CRESTED CRANES, 1957
Gouache with blue and black
ink, 16⅛ × 11⅝"

THE PORTAL OF DEATH AT ST PETER'S IN ROME

The execution of the portal for the Vatican could be delayed no longer, especially as Pope John was urging the completion since he hoped to inaugurate it at the beginning of the second Vatican Council in February 1962. At this stage Manzù had, in fact, not even begun the real work. Early that year his paternal friend, Monsignor Giuseppe De Luca, who had been closely connected with the project since its inception, became seriously ill; the Pope visited him in hospital. When the prelate died on 18 March 1962 the artist begged papal permission to dedicate the portal to the deceased, which he received without hesitation. It was not until the end of the year that preparations had reached the point where Manzù could start work on the portal itself.

Manzù's friend of many years, Cesare Brandi, has said that during the work on the portals — which took eighteen months from the end of 1962 to the beginning of 1964 — the artist achieved a distance from his work 'which almost bordered on animosity. Being forced to tackle themes to which he was bound by general feeling but not by specific faith, a kind of cold rage was released in him which explains the violent directness of creation and the gripping freshness of execution.' But it is not impossible that external circumstances contributed as much to this animosity as spiritual conflicts, especially since Manzù had long ceased to connect the treatment of biblical themes with definite religious feelings. Although the artist liked to muse over a project for many years, he was in this case not only contractually bound to specific dates but, in the meantime, had also lost enthusiasm in the project for several other reasons. Even the commission of the work was connected with circumstances which upset him.

The competition for two doors of St Peter's had been announced on 1 July 1947. Manzù submitted a plaster model for an entire door, and a detail, a wax bust of a saint, later destroyed. In March 1948 a jury examined the entries and decided to invite twelve artists to another competition, for which they had to submit a complete design with studies of details for one portal and a drawing for another one. Manzù was among these twelve sculptors and prepared a new, complete project (since then cast in bronze and now in the Blanc collection in Rome) plus two reliefs in original size, representing the deaths of St Xavier and Gregory VII (now in the Lampugnani collection in Milan). The brush and ink sketch for the second door — closely related to a variant of the 1947 project that was not submitted — is still in the possession of the artist.

While Manzù was awaiting the decision of the committee, Monsignor De Luca published a brochure on Manzù's designs which appeared — anonymously — in Rome in 1949. In April 1950 three artists were chosen for the execution of three portals — instead of the two originally planned — but Manzù did not receive the letter with the official commission until 25 January 1952. Brandi has pointed out that the two competitions already meant a humiliating delay for Manzù and that it would have been a 'satisfaction for him to be commissioned for the work instead of having been approached with a group of others'. This is particularly true since in the meantime a fourth door, the Porta Santa, had been commissioned from another sculptor without a competition and had been inaugurated at Christmas 1949. Added to this is the 'lowering of the artistic significance of Manzù's own work by the banal commissions for the other portals of the basilica'.

Nevertheless Brandi rightly considered the commission as a sort of reparation for the antagonistic attitude of the Vatican towards Manzù when he exhibited his relief series 'Cristo nella nostra umanità' in Milan in 1941, for which Brandi himself had written the introductory text. Moreover it was still an honour for the son of a poor sexton from Bergamo to be entrusted with a portal for the greatest church of the Catholic world. Regardless of some doubtless unpleasant and discouraging side issues, the commission was a recognition of Manzù's artistry, and his name would now be linked forever with the works of Bramante, Michelangelo, Raphael and Bernini. The sculptor was offered not only the rare opportunity to create an important work but to see it placed in a unique frame where it would be seen and admired daily. Is it not after all posterity which makes its merciless choice between a 'banal commission' and a true masterpiece?

Manzù was well aware of these circumstances. That his project underwent many changes in the course of the years was not least due to the fact that he wanted to surpass himself, all the more so since the magnitude of the task often filled him with doubts and caused dejection. The alterations which Manzù had undertaken since 1947 were of manifold kinds: first they were concerned with the division of the large area into diverse rectangles of varying format for the representation of individual scenes (the original plan had provided sixteen completely identical fields); secondly, they pertained to artistic factors, the first design with an overabundance of decorative elements and lettering being discarded for a very much calmer composition (the art-nouveau-like arabesques of intertwined olive branches having in the meantime been used on the reverse side of the Salzburg portal); lastly these changes are particularly related to iconographic problems, especially after John XXIII had agreed to a basic chance of the leitmotiv. With 'Death' as the general theme it was possible to choose quite different subjects for the various reliefs. There were also practical questions in which the experience gathered in Salzburg played an important role. This is true not only of the complicated casting but also of the effective combination of high and low relief.

The first and most important decision was to divide the surface of the doors into distinctly separated upper and lower sections in which, as in Salzburg, each of the upper parts is filled with a single, tall relief, while the lower ones consist of four smaller fields grouped together. In Salzburg each of the lower portions features a single almost square relief, but a considerable neutral area extends between the large upper and smaller lower section. In the new portal this area is much reduced and door-knobs of ears of corn and grapevine tendrils are placed in the centre (instead of being pushed to the inner edge as in Salzburg). As a consequence of this division the four smaller reliefs are approximately at the eye-level of the observer so that they appear almost like the illustrations of a book opened before him, whereas the two large reliefs are placed not only high above him but depict scenes which seem far removed from him and which he perceives only in the distance. Taking this distance into account, the figures in the upper reliefs are on a much larger scale than the lower ones.

The lower edge of the doors had originally been designed to show a series of buckles in high relief but these were replaced by animals as in the Salzburg portal, this time symbolic of death. These are an unspecified dead bird, a dormouse, a hedgehog, an owl, a tortoise with a snake and a raven, the last being the only animal already depicted at Salzburg. It is characteristic of the unusual patience and care of the artist that he made no fewer than twenty-four fully worked out studies of these six details, of which he later destroyed ten. As with the animals so also with the reliefs; a great many variants were created.

After receiving the final commission for the Vatican portal, Manzù decided in 1954 to change radically the designs submitted in 1948 and 1949. The new project filled the two upper fields with the Ascension of Christ and the Assumption of the Virgin, while the lower eight reliefs were planned as episodes from the life of Cain and Abel, Abraham,

STUDY FOR 'VARIATIONS ON A THEME', c. 1958
Pen and ink with watercolou
11⅝×8"

Moses, John the Baptist, as well as of Saints Joseph, Stephen, Francis Xavier and Gregory VII. Those themes which were still retained in the extensively altered model of 1958 (as for instance the Assumption of the Virgin) were later completely transformed to fit harmonically into the new overall design.

The project of 1958, which came very close to the final portal, was created after Manzù had received permission to choose death as the general theme. With the aid of Monsignor De Luca a new iconographic plan was worked out which led to the selection of the following scenes: for the two upper fields the Assumption of the Virgin and Christ's Descent from the Cross with a mourning figure of a clothed Eve (she had already appeared naked on one of the reliefs of 1939); for the eight smaller areas, in the upper row: the death of Abel, the death of St Joseph, the death of the arch-martyr St Stephen and the death of Gregory VII; for the lower row non-biblical themes were decided upon, namely illustrations of forms of death occurring in everyday life: death by violence (reminiscent of Manzù's relief of 'Death of a Partisan' of 1956), death in the water, death in the air and death on earth. Among the scenes omitted after having been included in the project of 1954 was the beheading of John the Baptist (for which I had seen so many studies in Manzù's studio), but some of these had in the meantime been used for the Salzburg portal. While Manzù was working on the lower reliefs, the aged Pope John XXIII died on 3 June 1963. The artist requested permission to replace 'Death in the Water' with a representation of the deceased, which was granted. He did not show the pope on his deathbed, however, but kneeling in reverent prayer.

Pope John appears twice on the portal of death. On the reverse, which was originally intended to be devoid of ornament, Manzù created, at the request of the Holy Father, a frieze to immortalize the calling of the second Vatican Council. The enthroned pope is shown during the opening of the council receiving the homage of the African cardinal Rugambwa. Both John XXIII and the African prelate are represented by astonishingly lifelike portraits although Rugambwa, who did not belong to the Curia, never sat for his likeness. Manzù selected this particular priest because the pope had spoken of him with special affection while the artist was drawing and modelling the preliminary sketches for the official bust of John XXIII. To the left of this group, a long row of unidentifiable church dignitaries extends across the whole width of both doors. On the left edge of the right-hand door (the door on which the seated pope is shown) appears a priest apparently leaving the scene, an allusion to the death of Monsignor De Luca which had occurred a short while before. Not far from it is the inscription, authorized by the pope (himself since deceased): 'A don Giuseppe De Luca questa porta della morte dedica Giacomo Manzù 1963' ('This portal of death is dedicated to Don Giuseppe De Luca by Giacomo Manzù, 1963').

Although De Luca's influence on the creation of the portal was great, there can be no doubt that the benevolence and understanding of the pope, and even the impatience with which he followed the artist's work, contributed decisively to bringing Manzù finally to the point of laying aside everything else and devoting himself exclusively to the portal of St Peter's in the autumn of 1962. Notwithstanding frequent attacks of doubt during the long preparation, the decision no longer to prevaricate seemed to give him the strength to carry through the immense undertaking without pausing for breath, so to speak.

The large and small reliefs now followed each other in an uninterrupted sequence, each one requiring intensive efforts before the final version was achieved. But however great the care taken in the individual scenes, his main concern was with the organization of the whole. The proportion of the fields and their distribution were fundamentally of much greater importance than thematic questions, especially since Manzù could — as in Salzburg — treat iconographic problems with a certain independence. Once having reached a satisfactory arrangement for the large area of the doors, he did not permit himself the slightest deviation from it. When, for instance, it was found during the execution that certain measurements of the portals had been taken incorrectly, Manzù preferred changing the size of the lower reliefs to the much simpler solution of altering the distance of these fields from the outer rim of the door. In this instance, as in many others, it meant submitting himself to the rules of the overall arrangement which he had established only after a long search. Although this arrangement was nothing but a scaffold into which his creations would be placed, it yet seemed of particular importance to the artist, because the reliefs could only have an independent — and at the same time interdependent — existence if they were to fit organically into the chosen framework. This frame also extended in depth, inasmuch as it consisted of two superimposed layers: the plane of the portal itself, and that of the individual reliefs laid upon it. Thus the flat backgrounds of the reliefs are prevented from melting into the plane of the doors, from which only the knobs of ears of corn and grapevine shoots, and the animals on the lower edge, arise in high relief. (In Salzburg there had been no such separate layers.)

Although the individual representations of the smaller reliefs largely fill the squares assigned to them, the edges are less frequently broken by details than in Salzburg. This is probably explained by the very fact that in Salzburg the level of the door is identical with that of the reliefs, separated from them by scratched lines only. By raising the fields of relief from the portal, and isolating these further by the shadows thus created, each relief gains an independent and enclosed space. At the same time too great a separation of these reliefs placed above and beside each other had to be avoided. The artist achieved the necessary unity by sacrificing all indication of perspective in individual reliefs (with the exception of the chair of the dying woman, whose child, on the other hand, is by no means 'thrust' into the background but is clearly on the same plane as herself). Indeed, Manzù chose mainly single figures, but even when dealing with two figures their intersections are reduced to a minimum of apparent depth, so that events always appear to take place in a completely 'empty' or at least indeterminate space. Due to the lack of a spatially defined background it seems as if all scenes are developed on the same plane, and there is no conflict between diverging perspectives.

Thanks to this ingenious composition the artist not only managed to solve the problem created by the unavoidable succession of various scenes, but also to lighten as much as possible the immensity of the bronze mass. The large area is so animated that its natural weight no longer asserts itself. It is perhaps even more astonishing that the tenderness of the modelling of the reliefs is neither in dramatic contrast to the sheer mass nor stifled by it; their proportion and execution form a complete unity with the portal and impress the observer as such.

Glancing upwards one perceives two graceful angels flying to meet the Mother of God and lead her to heaven. The artist achieved the natural appearance of the richly-folded garments by experimenting with rags and bits of paper soaked in plaster to gain the unforced effect he desired. Due to the distance dictated by the height of the portal one can, however, see only the main lines of the gracefully fluttering material. The head of the upper angel practically disappears behind these folds which look almost like an abstract, free-floating form. The diagonal of the outstretched, sleeping Mary leads the eye inevitably to the relief on the right door, where it is continued in the arm of the man throwing the whole weight of his body on the tense rope on which the dead Christ is being lowered

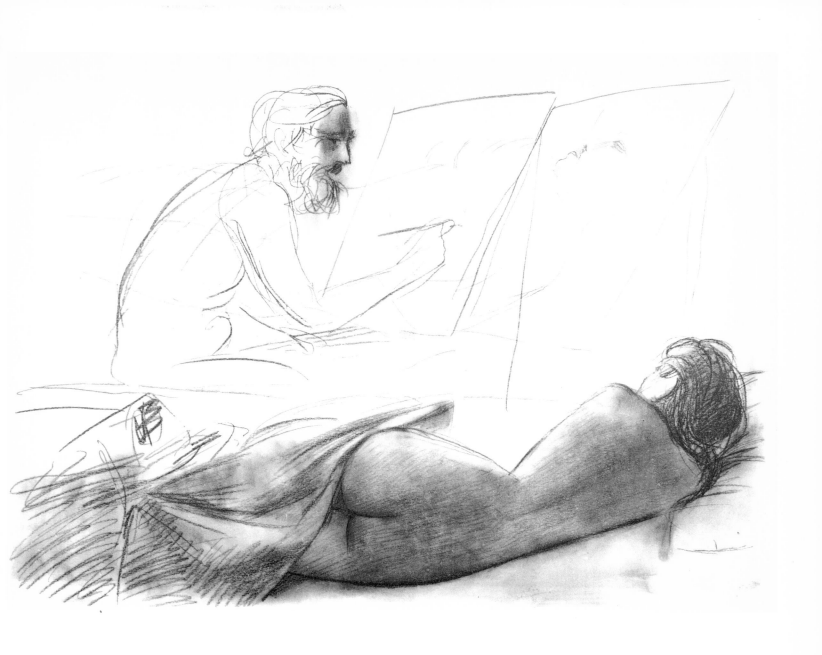

PAINTER AND MODEL, 1959
Pencil, 14⅛ × 18⅞"
Owned by the artist

from the cross. Although these lines are not unduly stressed, they do create a perceptible rhythm between the curve formed by the angels and the rope as well as the Saviour and his sunken head; they almost form a circle, the symmetrical order of which is consciously broken by the mourning Eve in the right-hand corner. Whereas the tragic-sublime events of these two reliefs can only be seen from afar, the lower scenes are spread before the viewer at a tangible distance; but here, too, he remains a witness without becoming involved in the various episodes. Manzù never seems to turn directly and dramatically to the observer in order to arouse his sympathy; he is satisfied to chronicle certain events without using the many traditional symbols of death — he is, indeed, consciously intent on softening as much as possible the usual expression of cruelty of 'the old man with a scythe'. A relief in which Cain's arm was raised to strike the help-lessly cowering Abel was replaced at the last moment by a variant in which the murderous onslaught is already over, and although the martyr's death of St Stephen is unmistakably symbolized by flying stones, one cannot see the perpetrators of this crime.

In several of the lower reliefs death comes almost as a release; he never appears in person. A tired Joseph, a stoned Stephen or a praying John XXIII accept their fate in solitude and with devout resignation. The types of death in everyday life, however, vibrate with a certain excitement, as if the contrast were intended to indicate that only saints can knock on the portal of eternity in peace and serenity, whereas ordinary mortals meet death with horror or even try to flee from him. (Manzù himself — whose health was suddenly threatened during his work on the portal — clings to life with every fibre of his being, not so much to enjoy it but to continue the work he feels called upon to accom-plish.) The whirlwind with which death in the air destroys his screaming victim clearly shows this fear of dying. In death by violence, on the other hand, all brutality is banished from the scene; the hanging corpse of the partisan is mourned by a woman whose lovely features are reminiscent of Inge. All theatrical gestures are avoided. She stands with lowered eyes and painfully distorted mouth, her fingers helplessly spread. Death is a judge against whose verdict there is no appeal.

Not only did Manzù avoid stressing the cruelty and horror of death in the individual com-positions, he also sought to lighten the darker aspect of his leitmotiv by his execution. The gentleness — one might almost say the tenderness — of the modelling through which the clay takes shape under his fingers, the subtle treatment of swelling forms, the im-pressively animated textures down to slight irregularities in which the hand of the artist makes itself felt even on theoretically flat surfaces, the sharp lines scratched in here and there which sparkle with life, the superb certainty with which a few carefully executed details are added to sparse outlines or summarily conceived contours — all these give evidence not only of a rare mastery but also of the intimate relationship between the artist and his work.

For a long time past religious art has not enjoyed that unity of form and content that it possessed in the Middle Ages. Today it addresses itself to two quite different realms: the aesthetic joy released by artistic creations and the pious beliefs kindled by its symbolism. To the same degree to which mysticism disappeared from everyday life, the art of the Church grew hollower. The religious works of many modern artists lack piety and trans-cendence even when they harbour artistic merits. Manzù is all the mor conscious of this situation as his own religious feelings are not tied to dogma but are rooted in his general concept of the world. This concept — based on intuition rather than on philosophic brooding — mirrors his whole life, from his poverty-stricken childhood in Bergamo and his first uncertain experiments right down to the fame he enjoys today. The many stages of the portal of St Peter's, the numerous discarded designs, and the countless preliminary studies prove how difficult Manzù made things for himself before he was satisfied with the expression he had given to his thoughts and feelings.

It is always most instructive to follow, step by step, the birth of a work of art and, if possible, to watch the artist during its creation. We possess a documentary film about this portal, made by Glauco Pellegrini, who filmed the various stages of the doors from the end of 1959, as well as the sculptor at work, particularly during the last phases in the studio and the foundry. One of the most fascinating scenes of the film occurred when Manzù was not conscious of being observed by the camera. With energetic movements and unbelievably dexterous, spontaneous modelling he had just finished a large relief in wet clay when he thought that shooting was over for the day and suddenly grasped a wire implement; before the horrified eyes of the observer he reduced the magnificent figure — still animated from his hands — with one vigorous stroke to a mere lump of clay. It is a breathtaking event of lightning speed, deeply moving and made bearable only because we know that the man who acts so barbarously can just as quickly create a new, and surely even more beautiful, work.

The layman generally knows nothing of such incidents nor of the hopes and disappointments that are connected with any work of art. The tourist who visits Rome or the pilgrim whose goal is the basilica of St Peter may never have heard of Manzù, but his portal will hardly escape their notice. Many, however, may not realize that this mighty portal has only recently been installed, for it fits most harmoniously into the grandiose architecture, and the tones of the new bronze alloy used in the casting blend splendidly with the surroundings. It is most important that this tremendous work is touched by a timelessness which is rarely encountered these days. Since no attempt was made to create something new and trail-breaking the observer understands the language and contents of feeling immediately. The modernity lies in the great simplicity of form, the sacrifice of all that is not essential, and in the purity of sentiment which is carried not so much by religious mysticism as by the deeply human feeling for the tragedy of those hours when life ebbs to a close. An artist at the height of his powers and means of expression drew on his own wounds and the bitter experience of bloody years of war to convey not so much the horrors and pathos of death, as the loneliness and dignity with which man meets his fate. He conceived death to be part of life and represented it with great tenderness. This explains why Carlo Levi, a friend of Manzù, could write of the portal:

'This is one of those works destined to bear witness to the real values of our age when experiments, polemics, trends and fashions bound up with contemporary life are past and forgotten.'

Levi pointed out that in this case, 'deprived of sin and therefore of redemption, Death appears in that unique moment, that fixed instant in which the violence of nature turns to harmony: a unity of expression which embraces the dead and the living, the victims, the witnesses and the killers.'

Early in 1964, when the actual work was finished, the artist turned to the foundry in Milan to which he had for many years entrusted the casting of his works. The bronze consisted of an alloy which Manzù had developed in cooperation with a scientist, but it was found subsequently that the proportions of the ingredients were faulty. After the first casting a second had to be made, different in melt but otherwise identical. Although the artist was not always present during the various phases of the casting, he followed the progress of this complicated task by telephone every day. The reliefs were eventually secured into the two door frames which had been completed since 1962. A final, and not inconsiderable, problem was the transport of the huge pieces from Milan to Rome. On 28 June 1964 the portal was solemnly inaugurated by Pope Paul VI.

CAMPO DEL FICO

While working on the portal Manzù had rented a small apartment from a titled Roman family. It lay in the quiet quarter of Aventino and next to the flat was an unused, narrow chapel with a very high ceiling in which he could work on the plaster models of the doors (part of Pellegrini's documentary film was shot there under considerable difficulties). The artist also had a large studio on the edge of Rome, but the great distance between his home and this studio made life difficult for him. His existence nevertheless was focussed exclusively on these two points, for Manzù found no need to take part in the intellectual — much less the mundane — life of the Eternal City. Although he had met in Rome some of his pre-war Milanese friends, such as Renato Guttuso, Carlo Levi and Cesare Brandi, he joined them but seldom. While he did feel well entertained whenever he participated in noisy evening meals in crowded trattorias where he and his companions were joined by authors such as Moravia, film directors like Antonioni or De Laurentiis or actresses like Monica Vitti, it always required a special occasion to get Manzù into this stimulating society. Left to himself he preferred to stay at home. When receiving visitors from abroad the artist is almost helpless, completely ignorant as he is of the nightspots his guest may wish to see.

Since Manzù did not participate in the real life of the city, he suffered from all the disadvantages of the metropolis while gaining none of its advantages. The wealth he now enjoyed made him neither arrogant nor did it help to surmount his shyness; his need for social contact was and remains small. It is not surprising then that he began to yearn increasingly for a house in the country. When Milan had become unbearable during his youth he had found refuge in Bergamo. Now he was no longer drawn there, although he continues to be fond of his home town. What he longed for — and what was to be the fulfilment of his dreams — was an isolated house in the country, with a large studio, where he could live and work without completely turning his back on the city.

Manzù thus began to look for a suitable place in the vicinity of Rome and found one in the direction of the sea, within about an hour's drive by car. The site he discovered was a slightly elevated, bare terrain near a village, from where one can see the distant shore while the surrounding farms are not obtrusive. It is a solitary place which in most directions dominates the neighbourhood. The elongated one-storey house which was built there has overhanging eaves and a thatch of reeds that move slightly in the wind, reminiscent of South Sea huts. The comparatively few rooms are spacious and well-lit, sparsely furnished and floored with coloured tiles that look like gay carpets. Through the windows one sees the extensive grounds; these have been planted with a number of trees which will soon give a more pleasing prospect without separating the house too much from the distant, hilly landscape.

Not far away are some smaller buildings with lodgings for gardeners and servants, as well as an impressive structure which Manzù's friends jokingly declare is large enough to serve as an aeroplane hangar. This is his studio, his first real one, for up to now he has always had to make do with rooms which did not meet his demands and only became his workshops through expediency. The tremendous scale of the studio proves the optimism of the almost sixty-year-old artist, who, with unconcealed satisfaction, was now started to fill the impressive but empty space with projects and new works.

When entering this great hall one immediately notices, hanging on the right-hand wall, the old, slightly fragile chair with the woven seat which has so often appeared not only in the sculptures of the seated nude girl but in so many other works as well. It even became a subject itself on occasion, and served repeatedly for etchings and still-life sculptures when loaded with fruit and vegetables. In one corner stands the plaster of the elongated dancer which now graces a fountain in Detroit. Since the artist has up to now adopted the rule not to have more than one cast of each work made, one does not find the profusion of plaster models and forms met with in the studios of most sculptors.

Manzù's new workshop consists of an extended, well-lit hall, joined at right angles at the far end to another long, bare room; a wall divides them. A small, separate studio is arranged in the furthest part of the second room and comfortably equipped with furniture and a stove; it is also fitted with built-in cupboards holding drawers. Here the artist can draw and paint or occasionally prepare etchings or lithographs (which he does not print himself, however). His graphic output is not inconsiderable. In the middle 'forties, after a few early works, he created more than sixty etchings for Virgil's G e o r g i c s. Since 1957 there have been perhaps a dozen further etchings, of which an edition of twelve is usually printed. His first lithographs originate from 1953 and 1954 and are illustrations for Quasimodo's I l f a l s o e v e r o v e r d e; of the twenty-seven lithographs which he created for it — among them several reminiscent of his reliefs — only seven accompanied Quasimodo's text when it was published in Milan in 1954. A series of lithographs dating from 1960 deals exclusively with the theme 'Artist and Model', of which Manzù had done a number of oils between 1957 and 1962, having previously devoted a few reliefs to the subject. He also treated this group in several free-standing sculptures, so that this subject has been created by him in black and white as well as in colours, in the round as well as on a plane; this again proves the intensity and perseverance with which Manzù devotes himself to the themes which inspire him.

Almost no graphic work came into being while the artist was concentrating on the portal of St Peter's. The only 'distraction' which he permitted himself was the supervision of the work on his new house and studio, the erection of which took a whole year. A few months after the inauguration of the Vatican doors, on 15 October 1964, Manzù moved into 'Campo del Fico', the 'grove of fig trees'.

When I visited him there in the spring of 1965 the studio was no longer bare. Besides the plaster model for the Detroit fountain (which is the last version of the series of 'Dance Steps' inspired by Inge), a large number of variants for the reliefs of the 'Portal of Death' were displayed on wooden scaffolding (they were exhibited in Venice in 1964 and in New York towards the end of 1965). In the meantime Manzù had refashioned a relief for Rocke-feller Center originally intended for the portal of the Salzburg cathedral. It is of a mother and child and now replaces the Fascist emblems of the Italian building which had been kept hidden for nearly twenty-five years. The artist thus is publicly represented in two cities of the United States, an honour which Milan, almost his second home, has not yet granted him. At that time there was also a large design for a church door in his studio; commissioned for Rotterdam, it varies widely in subject from the portals he has already created. Yet Manzù hopes soon to finish all the commissions he has already accepted so as to be able to dedicate himself to various projects he has dreamed of for years.

Since Manzù's work is closely interwoven with his life, and since his life proceeds with a quietude and withdrawal corresponding to the nature and characteristics of the artist, there are no sharp breaks or digressions in either his life or his work. The logical sequence of his creations is determined by the development of a creative man who, because of the slowness with which his plans mature, always thinks — whether he wants

PORTRAIT OF INGE, 1960
Pencil, 16½×11⅝"
Owned by the artist

STUDY FOR AN ICE SKATER, 1958
Pastel, $19\frac{1}{4} \times 12\frac{5}{8}$"
Owned by the artist

to or not — of the next work while completing the sculpture on which he is engaged. In this uninterrupted chain each work seems to continue the preceding one, and if Manzù sometimes keeps returning to the same theme with a certain perseverance he resembles a brook which endlessly polishes its pebbles. This persistent polishing is a process that lacks all drama, indeed Manzù avoids anything that threatens to interrupt the harmony of his industrious everyday existence. His creativeness is an intimate process for which he must isolate himself completely. In his large new studio he will, as before, wrestle in solitude with himself and his materials. If he is sometimes attacked by doubts, they arise from the gap between a completed work and the high demands he makes on himself. Although he may occasionally lack sufficient distance from a particular piece, he will yet never stray from the direction he has taken. Unfalteringly he follows his own way, looking neither left nor right, uninfluenced by stylistic trends or the sensational successes of other artists, unshakably convinced in his belief that there is no other solution for him than the one to which his nature drives him.

Sure of himself and yet modest, Manzù has lately striven to give expression to the feelings and attitudes which seem important to him. 'I moved', he wrote to me, 'to the country completely of my own free will. When living out here, in the extended landscape with the sea on the horizon, I no longer feel the contrast between an inner and an outer world. My aspirations and yearning seem suspended in mid-air and take possession of me from time to time by adapting themselves to my work which is dedicated to imitating nature instead of leading to a [more independent and intellectual] creation, as should really be the case. That is why I consider myself an artisan. I am as I am, and despite my burning desire, my distress and my constant pondering about the man of today and his possibilities, which are so far removed from mine, I can do nothing else for I am by nature an inhibited man who is not really prepared to learn. On top of that it is no longer possible, at my age, to have knowledge grafted on to one, so to speak, although I know that even inherent instincts have to be fostered.

'When I compare the results of my endeavours with my far-off childhood dreams and my present-day intentions, then it seems to me that everything has stopped half-way. Just the same I start work early every day as if it were my first morning, and I find in work my daily task and my confirmation. I know that this is very little, but this is the only true and honest thing I can say of myself as a man and as a sculptor.'

Perhaps it will be considered later that the 'Portal of Death' was the acme of Manzù's work, and because its completion coincided with his removal to his new home there may be a tendency to speak of a new artistic phase. The artist himself is not aware of such a new phase, although he feels a certain satisfaction about having reached his goal and at the same time enjoys a sense of liberation since the work for the Vatican has been completed. It is to be expected that this will be expressed in an increased activity. Whilst looking forward to this moment of 'liberation', Manzù had already made some decisions which concern his past work as well as the future. To begin with, he plans to have not one but two casts made of his sculptures from now on, although he intends to differentiate the second cast from the first by slight variations. Most of the series, of which there are a more or less great number of variants, he now regards as definitely completed. This applies especially to the 'Cardinals', the 'Girl on a Chair' and the 'Dance Steps'; nor will there by any more versions of the 'Ice-skater', all the more so as Inge's sister Sonja has not posed for him since she outgrew childhood. Manzù is basically uninterested in portrait commissions. After the bust of John XXIII he recently completed the portrait of Kokoschka which had been in progress since 1960. He naturally does not deny himself the pleasure of undertaking a portrait now and again if a head particularly appeals to him. Thus he created further portrait busts of Inge from time to time and recently did the head of a young actor whom he had met through De Laurentiis.

Originally Manzù had intended to concern himself anew with the theme of the 'Painter and Model' which has preoccupied him for such a long time, and he had also wished to start a new series of dancers; this was to deal not with figures in the nude or dressed in closely fitting tights, but with ballerinas in little tarlatan skirts, such as he had already sketched on occasion. Instead he is now busy with two completely new projects: a 'Pair of Lovers' and a kind of 'Striptease' in which, however, the girl who is baring herself avoids displaying her body; there are already several small-scale variants of this series of a model undressing as well as of lovers in fond embraces. Finally Manzù would like to come to grips with the theme of his first eight reliefs of the 'Death of Christ', first done in 1939, and to create a group of twenty-two reliefs of the same format on this subject. This intention proves most clearly that it is fundamentally the artistic problems — much more than the political and polemical ones which were originally attached to this series and made their exhibition a contentious event — which prompt Manzù's return to certain of his favourite projects.

MEETING PICASSO

Since living at Campo del Fico, Manzù has only once interrupted his work there. Accompanied by his friend Guttuso he visited Picasso at Mougins in March 1965. This short visit, which gave him the greatest pleasure, confirmed his opinion that Picasso is the only true master among living sculptors. Despite the almost unbridgeable differences in their nature, or perhaps because of them, this meeting was a profound experience for Manzù. It brought him into contact with a temperament that is like an erupting volcano, ceaselessly spouting smoke and lava. The vigour of the old man who tirelessly produced works from all corners of his large house to show to his guests, who stood around for hours in a huge vestibule while they walked from one haphazardly placed sculpture to another, whose magnetic personality seemed to give a special dimension to the paintings, drawings and collages lying everywhere in heaps, all this seemed strange and yet attractive to Manzù. There is probably nothing so fascinating as watching this thickset, mercurial, almost eerie genius who touched everything, transformed everything, who broke all rules, discarded all traditions and constantly developed new forms without keeping to them for long, because fresh discoveries were always waiting. What seems remarkable is that Picasso in his sculptures, far more than in his paintings, expresses his astonishing sense of humour, even a tendency towards the playfully jocular which sometimes goes so far as to make one almost doubt whether he takes himself quite seriously. This does not mean, however, that he is not to be taken seriously by others, for Picasso is as pioneering in sculpture as he is in all other fields to which he has dedicated himself, because he combines a sure instinct for volumes with a most daring gift of invention.

Among modern sculptors three names are of importance to Manzù: Renoir, Brancusi and Picasso. He admires Renoir's fullness of form, Brancusi's poetry, and is impressed by the enormous vitality of Picasso which can be felt even when a work has not been completely successful. As far as Giacometti is concerned, Manzù prefers his paintings and drawings to his sculpture. Although Maillol was the first artist who appealed to Manzù, he now feels that his work — in contrast to the few sculptures of Renoir — no longer

BALLERINA, 1961
Pencil, 15¾ × 11⅛"
Owned by the artist

possess what might be called 'actuality'. That he feels such a creative force in Brancusi, on the other hand, shows not only his unusual objectivity — for his own work has not, and never has had, anything in common with this artist — but also his fundamental love of true originality.

It may seem at first glance as if Manzù did not really fit into this circle. He himself would admit freely that he is as far removed from the ingenious use of existing objects which Picasso often employs in his sculptures, as he is from Brancusi's tendency to detach his themes from nature and to bring them back to an 'arch' form, which in turn appears to be an accomplished product of nature. But this does not exhaust the task of contemporary sculptors.

Those looking back on our era from the future will probably find little of lasting value among the confusion of present artistic productions. Sculpture has never seen such radical changes, never before have so many new materials and novel techniques been available. Intoxicated with as yet unexploited possibilities which contributed their share in the final rupture with all tradition, contemporary sculptors stop at nothing. They break up forms, perforate them, shatter them or compress them; they solder and weld, they utilize metal scraps or bits of machinery, they potter around with wood, paper, string, wire, rags, old books, plaster casts and 'found' objects unless they are satisfied with 'ready-mades'. They feast on absurdities. They experiment with movement and even with sound, not to speak of colour. They often show great skill, display wit and inventiveness, strive for new textures, force their brutal will on materials or are ready to submit to them almost slavishly. They try everything and occasionally achieve considerable results, even though dexterity and a kind of high spirits sometimes hide the absence of real originality. They indulge in an orgy of the never-done-before without always asking themselves for how long accidents — which often come to their aid and produce many successful effects — can be a substitute for artistic conception. Only when this intoxication has evaporated completely will it be possible to see how many fertile seeds have been sown. That some extraordinary and promising forces are at work cannot be denied.

Since the pendulum of history swings from one extreme to another, it is more than possible that this trend of uninhibited freedom — which indicates a certain surfeit of nature — will be followed by one which will re-establish closer bonds with nature. New generations will then recognize with gratitude that these bonds were never completely severed because Giacomo Manzù, in his isolation, kept the classical traditions alive. Obeying an inner necessity, he avoided participating in the experiments of his contemporaries and letting himself be led astray by the charms of the unusual. Instead he preferred to follow his own feelings and observations, which was more difficult than it may seem. Just as Rodin was once accused of having cast one of his male figures directly from the model, so Manzù is accused in some circles of keeping too close to nature. One could almost say that it requires more courage nowadays to remain faithful to nature than to turn one's back on her and pursue the abstract. (That Manzù himself fully recognizes the justification of such tendencies can be seen from his admiration of Brancusi.)

Manzù naturally kept aloof from all academic conventions and routines and relied completely on the creative instinct based on his own experiences. He avoids all theories and prefers to observe the world around him with passionate and tender intensity. The men, women and children who are the centre of his work are not only seen with an eye for configuration, but their expressions, their pain or joy, their sensuality or shyness have been interpreted without the use of anecdotal methods. Manzù penetrates so deeply into the feelings of these people that his statues — freed from all trivialities — appear timeless;

they are therefore perhaps not so much witnesses of our epoch as of his masterly creative force. Whether dealing with cardinals or dancers, biblical themes or naked children, he always knows how to transmit his concept in a language of pure form which appeals directly to the observer so that he can immediately participate in the perception of the artist.

When one watches Manzù in his new studio, talking about his plans or analyzing his work, one cannot escape the impression that here is a man who does not suffer at all by being completely dependent on himself. With a calm certainty, based on things already achieved, he dedicates himself to the only task he knows, namely to give form and thus permanence to his perceptions and slowly nurtured intentions. With an equal confidence he faces the future, for this task, to which he knows himself called by fate, is a never ending one.

PORTRAIT STUDY OF SONJA, 1962
Pencil

STUDY FOR 'GIRL PLAYING' (PLATE 91), 1955
Red ink
Coll. James N. Goodman, Buffalo, N. Y.

PLATES

Circus Scene, 1932
Wrought copper, c. $31^{1}/_{2} \times 21$"
Coll. L. A. Kolker, New Jersey

Weathercock, 1931
Wrought copper, h. 15³/₄″
Catholic University, Milan

Figure, 1931
Wrought copper, h. 12³/₄″
Owned by the artist

4

Annunciation, 1931
Polychrome stucco, 27¹/₂×21⁵/₈″
Coll. Manfredi Grosso, Milan

Entombment, 1932
Wrought silver, 15³/₄ × 13³/₄″
Coll. Zappettini, Milan

6
Female Head, 1935/36
Wax, h. 11″
Coll. Guasco, Turin

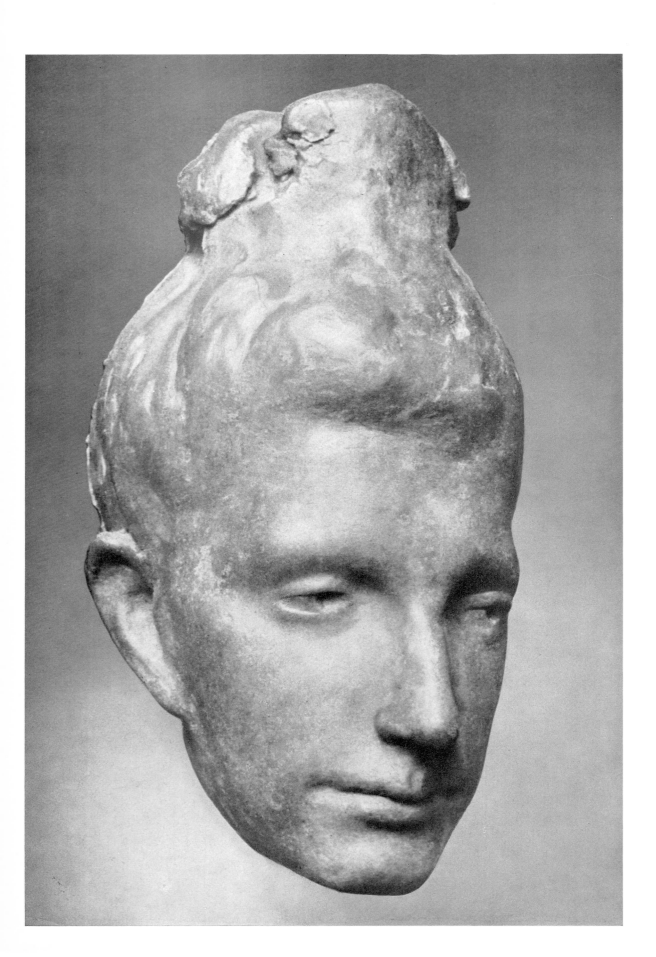

Study for a Saint Sebastian, 1934
Detail, bronze, h. 21⁵/₈″
Private coll., Milan

Portrait of Carla, 1936
Wax, h. 6¹/₄″
Coll. Lampugnani, Milan

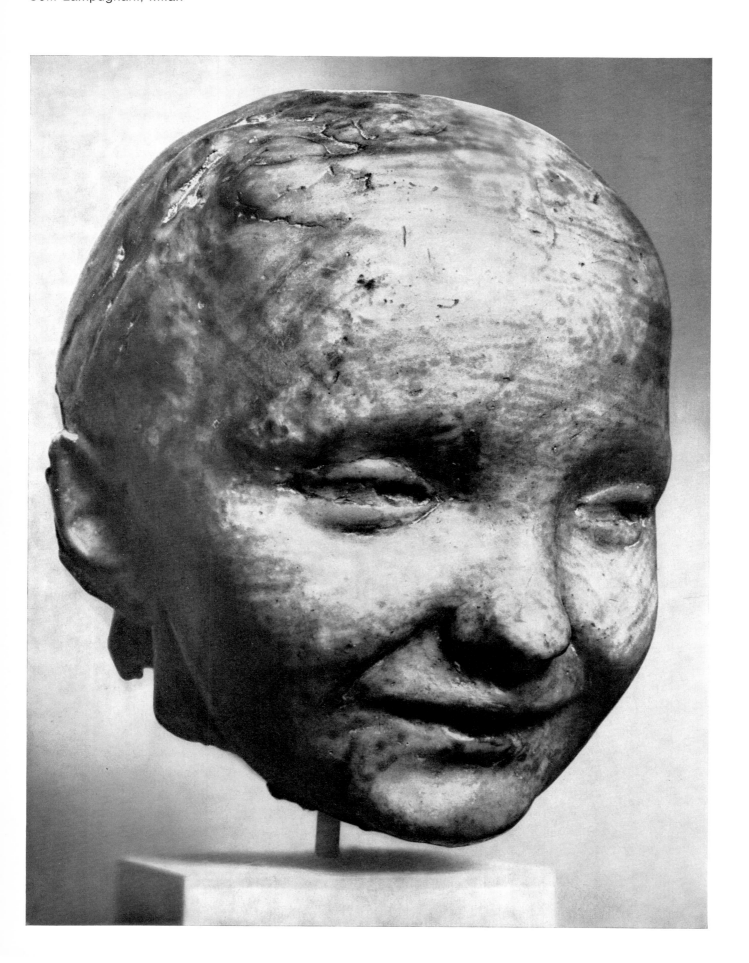

Portrait of the Artist's Wife, 1935
Wax, h. 8¼″
Private coll., Rome

10
Woman Putting on a Stocking, 1936
Bronze, h. 13³/₄″
Coll. Cassani, Milan

11
Susanna, 1937
Wax, h. 13³/₄″
Galleria Nazionale
d'Arte Moderna, Rome

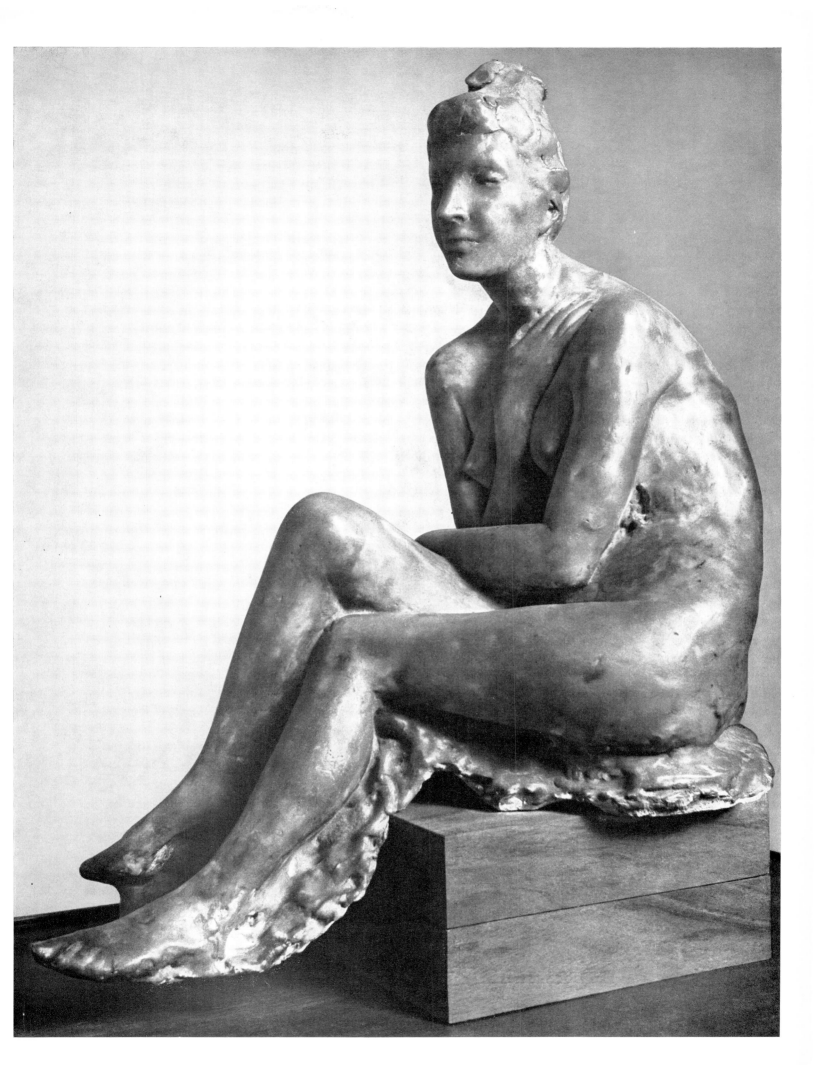

12
David, 1938
Bronze, h. 18⁷/₈″
Coll. Lampugnani, Milan

Man Bending, 1936
Bronze, h. 11″
Coll. Countess Pecci-Blunt, Rome

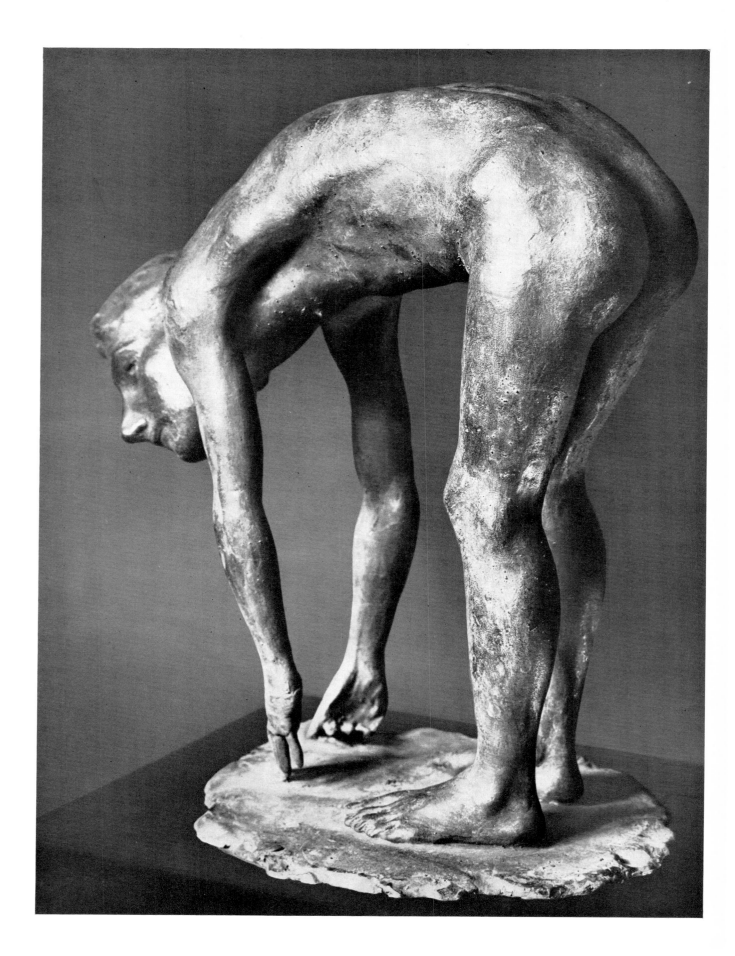

14

Bust of a Young Girl, 1947
Bronze, h. 12⁵/₈″
Coll. Lampugnani, Milan

Portrait of Signora Vitali, 1938/39
Detail, bronze, h. 25⁵/₈″
Coll. Lamberto Vitali, Milan

Francesca, 1942
Bronze, h. 3'7$^{1}/_{4}$"
Coll. Baroness Anita Blanc, Rome

Bust of a Girl at a Window, 1943
Bronze, h. 13$^3/_4$''
Private coll., Milan

Portrait of a Child, 1940
Bronze, h. 9''
(Photograph of the original plaster)
Coll. Rimoldi, Cortina

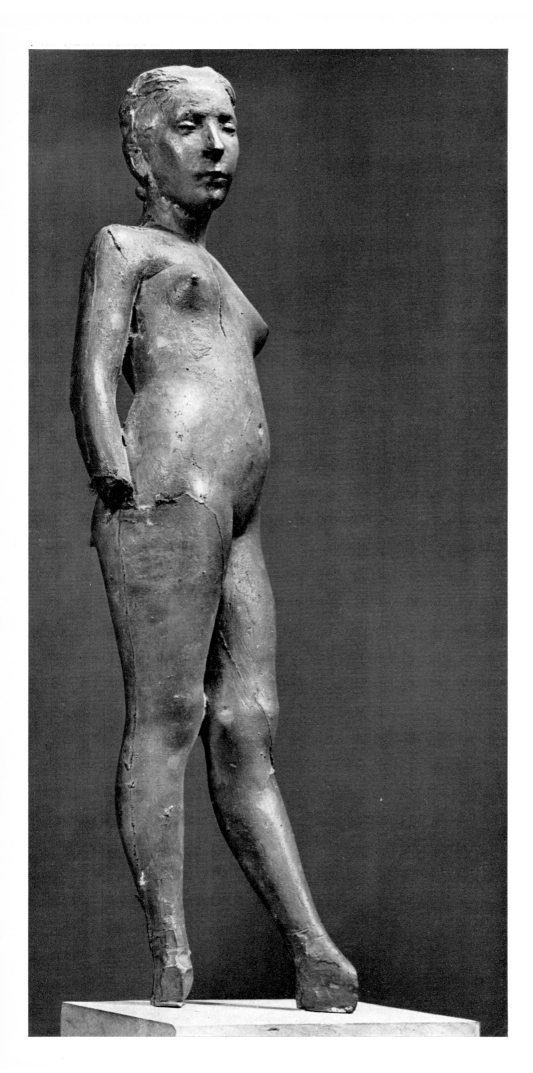

Nude of a Young Girl, 1941
Bronze, h. 15″
Coll. Dado Ruspoli, Rome

22

Dance Step, 1943
Bronze, h. 16¹/₈″
Private coll., Padua

23

Study for a Judgment of Salomon, 1943
Bronze, h. 8⅝"
Coll. Gualino, Rome

Standing Woman, 1946
Bronze, h. 15″
Coll. Gatti, Rome

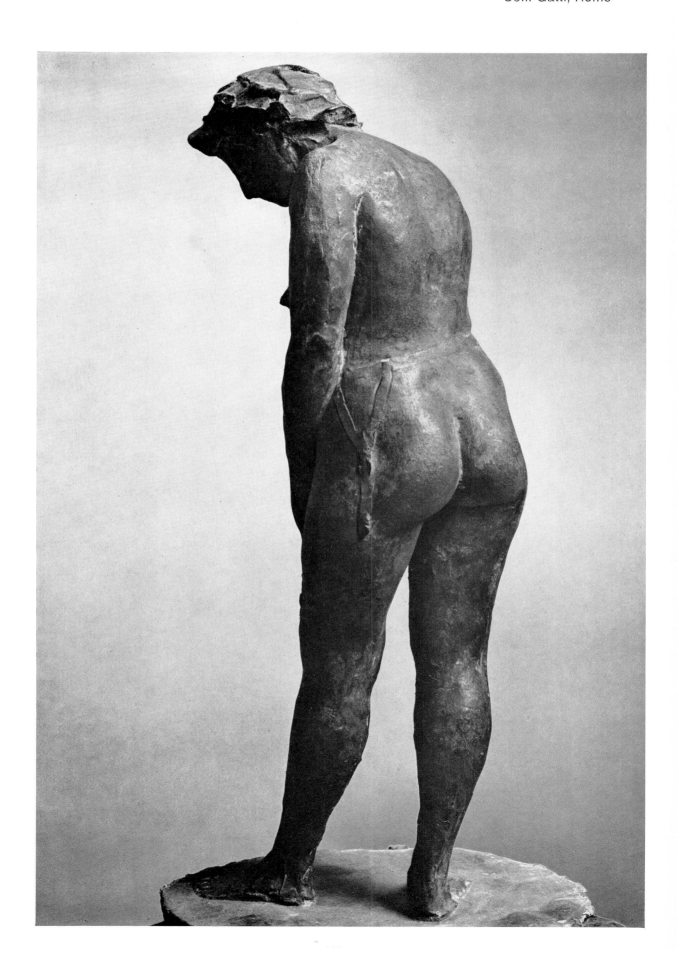

25

Young Girl Playing, 1953
Bronze, h. 19⁵⁄₈″
Schoolcamp, Wiesbaden

Bronze, h. 23⅝"
Child Playing, 1942
Coll. Ballini, Milan

Bust of a Woman, circa 1948
Bronze, h. 17⁵/₈″
Private coll., London

Bust of a Woman, 1947
Bronze, h. 27$^{1}/_{2}$''
Private coll., Milan

29

Head of a Woman, 1946
Terracotta, h. 9″
Coll. Luzzato, Buenos Aires

Mask, 1946
Terracotta, h. 8¹/₄″
Coll. Lampugnani, Milan

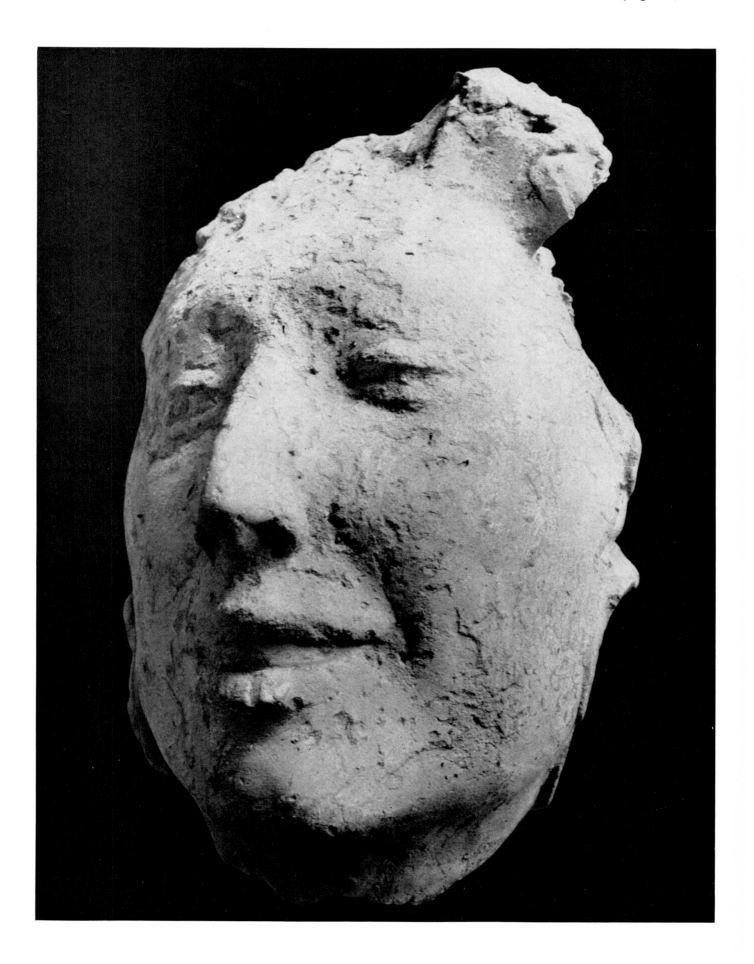

**Large Portrait
of a Lady, 1946**
See plate 33

32

**Self Portrait
with Model, 1946**
Bronze, h. 13³/₄″
Coll. Luzzato,
Buenos Aires

**Large Portrait of a Lady
in a Dressing Gown, 1946**
Detail of plate 31
Bronze, h. 5′5″
Coll. Lampugnani, Milan
Second cast: Museum of Modern Art, New York

Pieta, 1953
Bronze, h. 11³/₈″
Coll. Mrs. Werner E. Josten, New York

Cardinal, 1943
Bronze, h. 9⁷/₈″
Coll. Gualino, Rome

Kneeling Deacon, 1943
Detail of a Pieta
Bronze, h. 15″
Coll. Gualino, Rome

Cardinal, 1946
Bronze, h. 8⁵/₈″
Coll. Lampugnani, Milan

38
Child with Goose, 1947
Bronze, h. 19^5/$_8$"
Museo Revoltella, Trieste

Portrait of Pastorio, 1944
Bronze, h. 23⅝″
Coll. Pastorio, Milan

Head of a Woman, 1954
Bronze, h. 11″
Coll. Winand, Surrey, England

Head of a Woman, 1948
Bronze, h. 11″
Musée Royal des Beaux-Arts, Antwerp

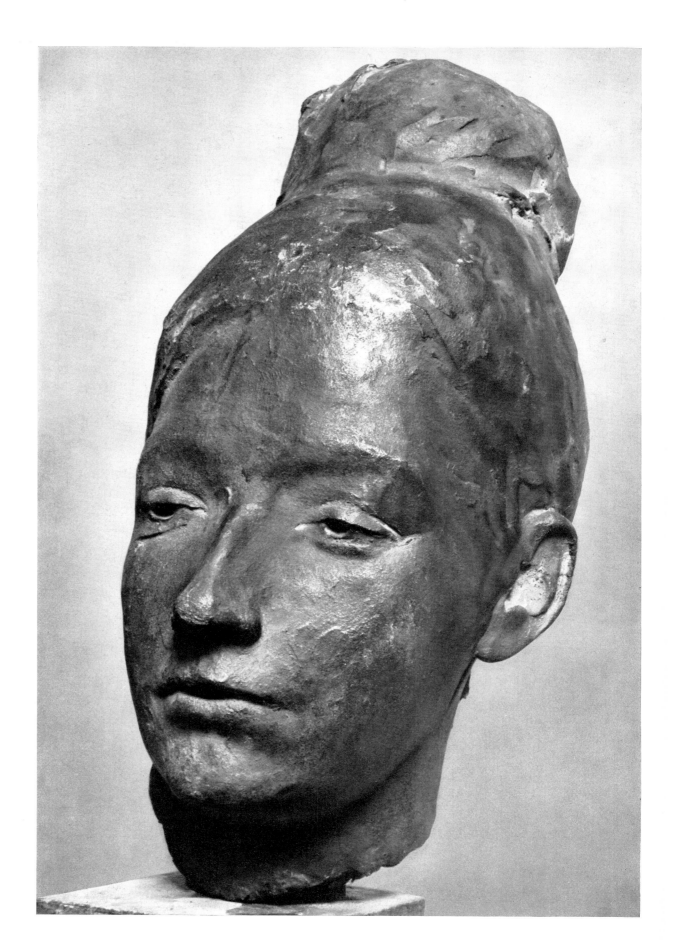

42

Bust of Caroline Wann, 1958
Bronze, h. 16$^{1}/_{2}$″
Coll. C. J. Wann, New York

Bust of a Woman, 1955
Bronze, h. 27¹/₂″
Private coll., London

Study for a Pieta, 1953
Bronze, h. 11³/₄″
Private coll., Graz

45

Study for a Saint Ambrosius, 1944
Bronze, h. 8⅝″
Coll. Gualino, Rome

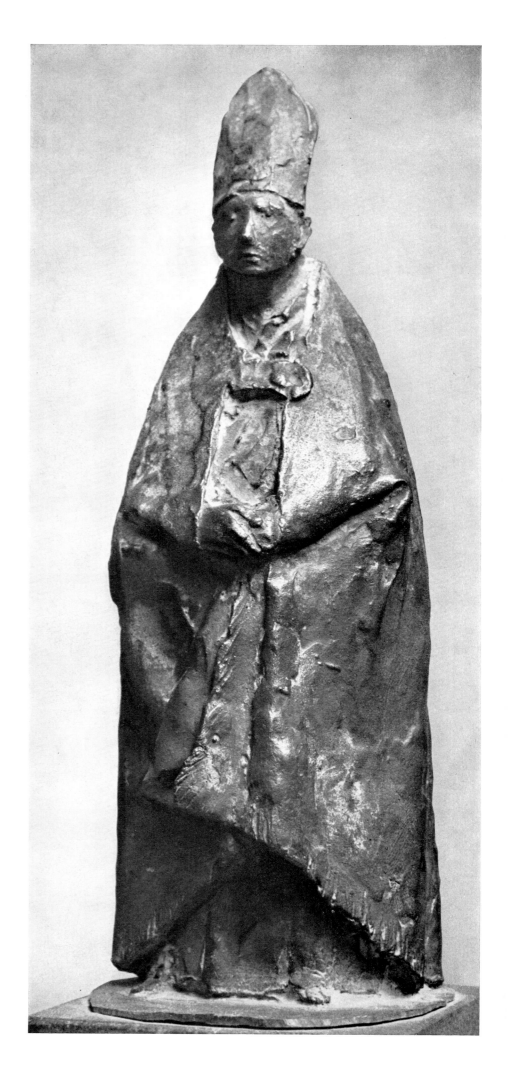

46
Cardinal, 1948
Bronze, h. 13³/₄″
Tate Gallery, London

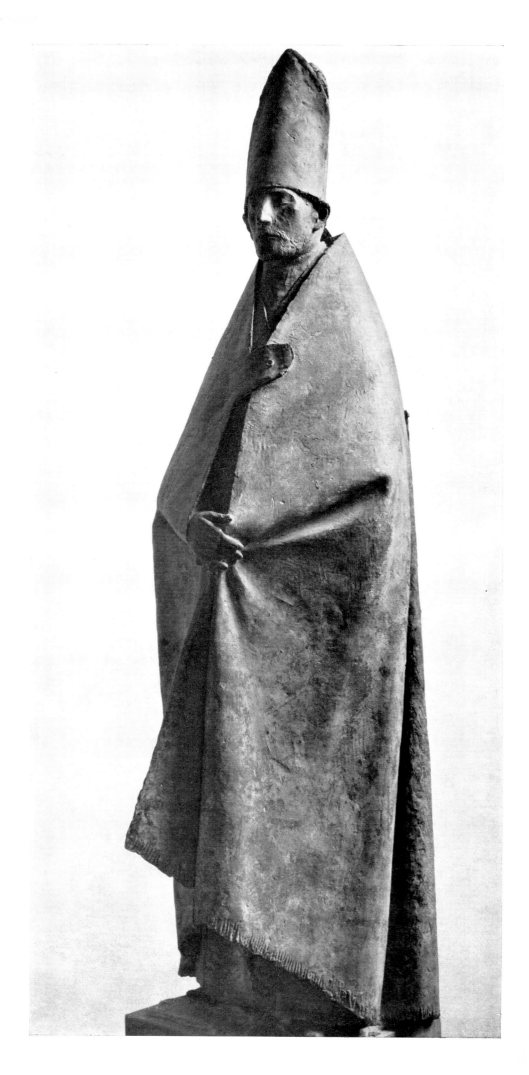

47
Cardinal, 1952
Bronze, h. 5′9″
Middelheimpark, Antwerp

Cardinal Lercaro, 1953
Bronze, h. 7′2⅝″
Basilica S. Petronio, Bologna

Cardinal, 1953
Bronze, h. 25⁵/₈″
Private coll., London

Head of Inge, 1954
Bronze, h. 10¼″
Coll. William Fleming, London

Head of a Woman, 1954
Bronze, h. 8⅝″
Museum, Verona

Young Girl on a Chair, 1955
Bronze, h. 3'5³/₈''
National Gallery, Toronto, Canada

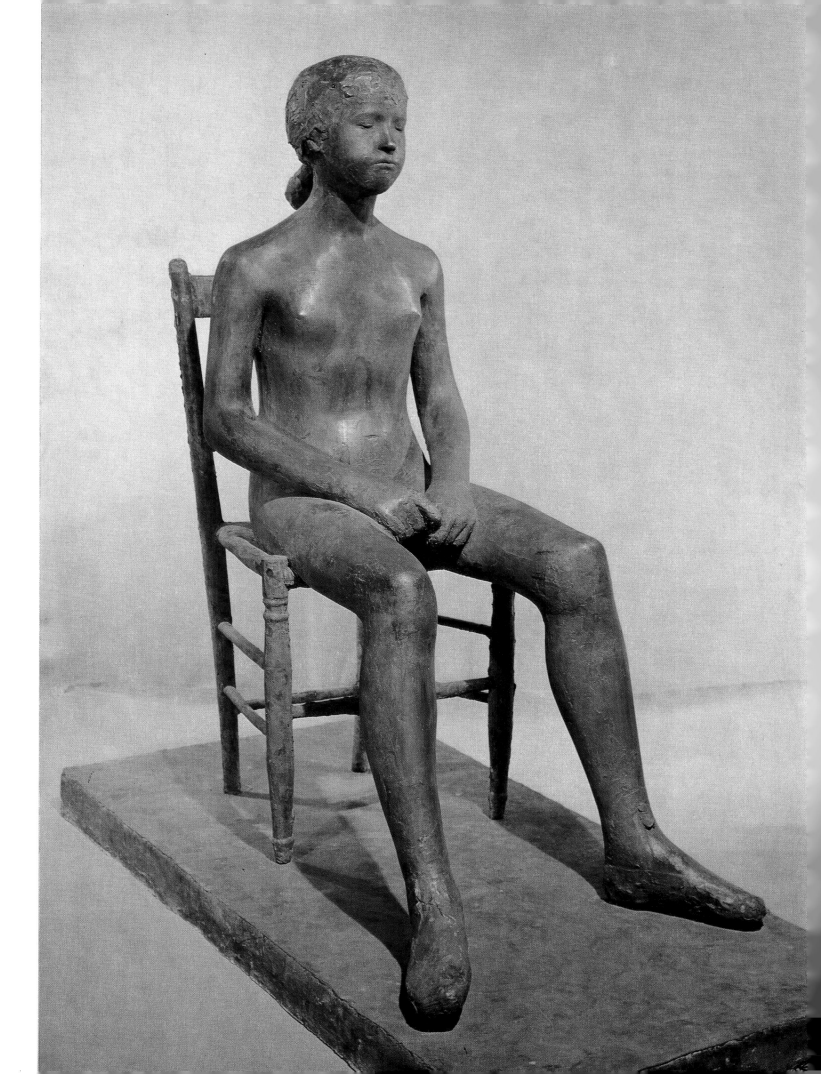

Young Girl on a Chair, 1955
Detail of plate 52

Crucifixion, 1951
High relief, bronze, $59 \times 50^3/_8''$
Middelheimpark, Antwerp

Entombment, 1951
High relief, bronze, 59 × 50³/₈″
Middelheimpark, Antwerp

Variations on the Theme of
„Cristo nella nostra umanità", 1947—1957
Low reliefs, bronze, c. 27¹/₂ × 19³/₄″
Owned by the artist

Variations on the Theme of
„Cristo nella nostra umanità", 1947—1957
Low reliefs, bronze, c. 27¹/₂ × 19³/₄″
Owned by the artist

Cardinal, 1954
Bronze, h. 15^3/$_8$''
Rhode Island School of Design, Providence, R. I., USA

Cardinal, 1950
Bronze, h. 27¹/₂″
Nationalmuseum, Oslo

68

Large Standing Cardinal, 1952
Bronze, h. 5′5″
Wallraf-Richartz Museum, Cologne
Variant in the Stadthus Tilburg, Holland

69

Seated Cardinal, 1955
Bronze, h. 7'2⅝"
Coll. Nathan Cummings,
Chicago

70

Cardinal, 1956
Detail, bronze, h. 7'2⅝"
Galleria Internazionale
d'Arte Moderna, Venice

Cardinal, 1953
Bronze, h. 12⅝''
Coll. Lampugnani, Milan

Cardinal, 1958
Bronze, h. 21¼″
Coll. Dr. Peter Müller, Vienna

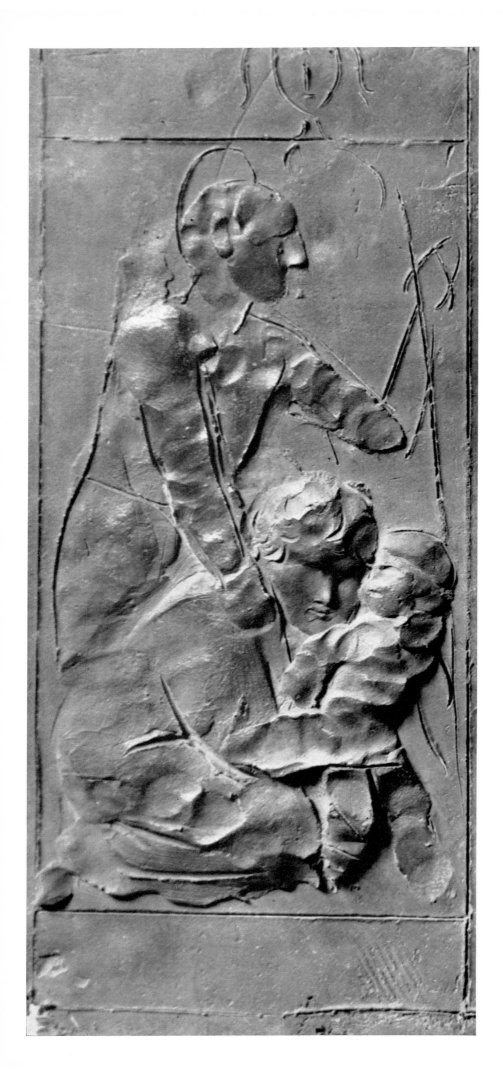

Saint Severin, 1958
Detail of a Study in three sections
for the Door of the Cathedral
in Salzburg
Relief, bronze, c. 21¹/₄ × 9¹/₂″
Coll. Joseph Hirshhorn, New York

74

Enchained Prisoner and Cardinal, 1956
Relief, bronze, 11 × 7⁷/₈″
Private coll., London

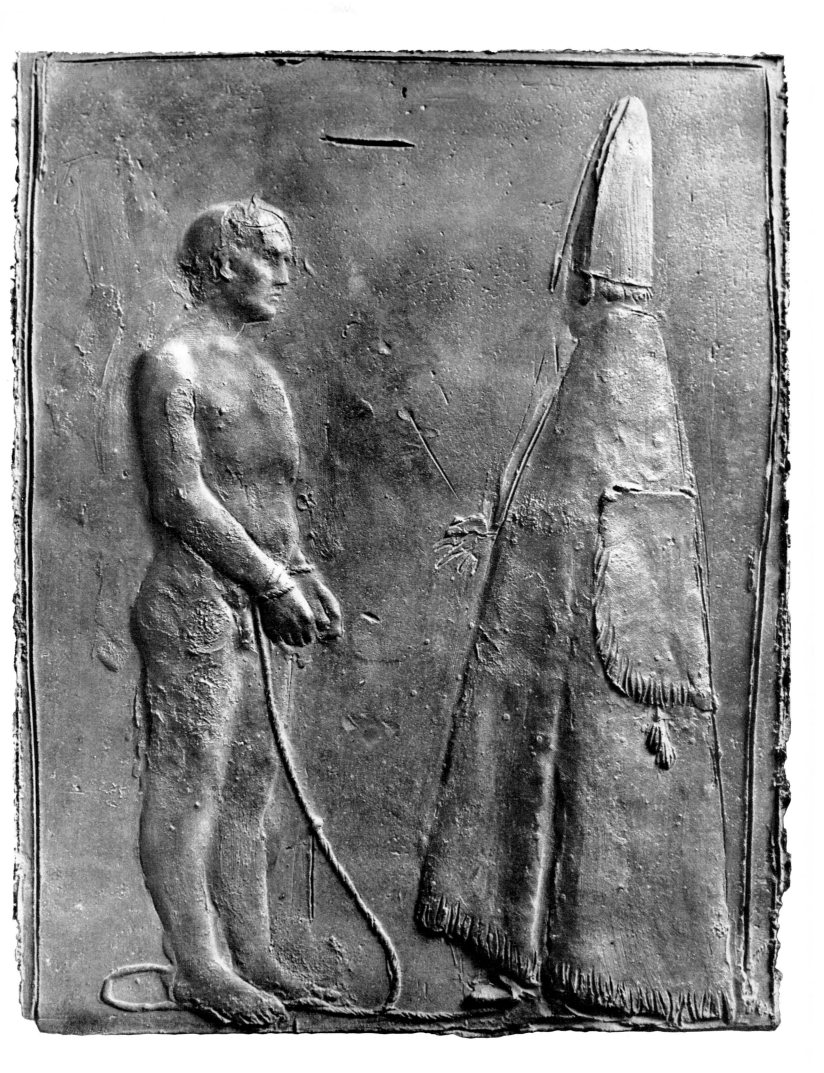

Painter and Model, 1942
High relief, bronze, h. c. 5′
Coll. Prof. Mayer, New York

**Grieving Woman
with Hanged Partisan, 1958**
High relief, bronze, h. 15³/₄″
Coll. Stern, Toronto

Dance Step, 1951
Bronze, h. 5'5''
Middelheimpark, Antwerp

78

Dance Step, 1951
Bronze, h. 5'10"
Coll. Herbert Mayer, New York

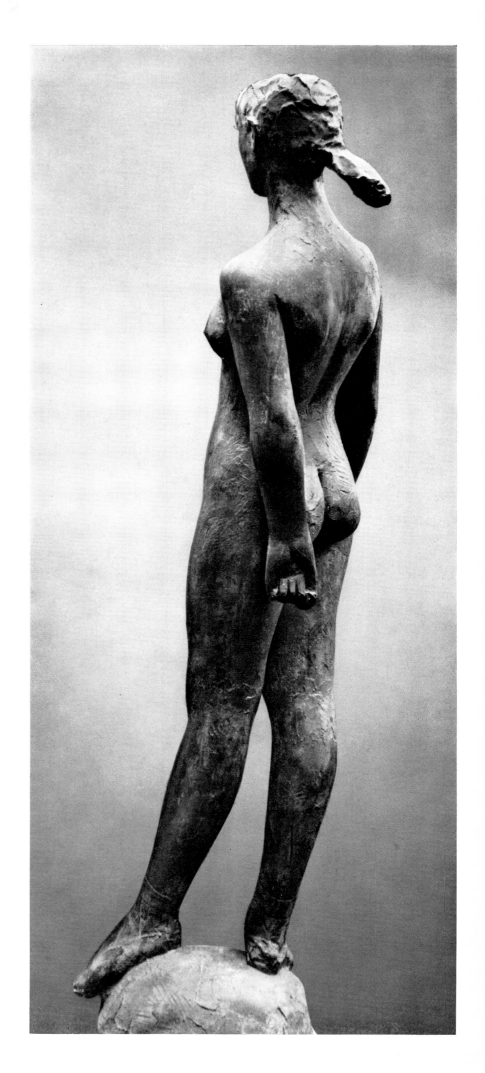

Dancer, 1955
Bronze, h. 27$^{1}/_{2}$″
Private coll., London

Dancer, 1953
Bronze, h. 23⅝"
Coll. Lampugnani, Milan

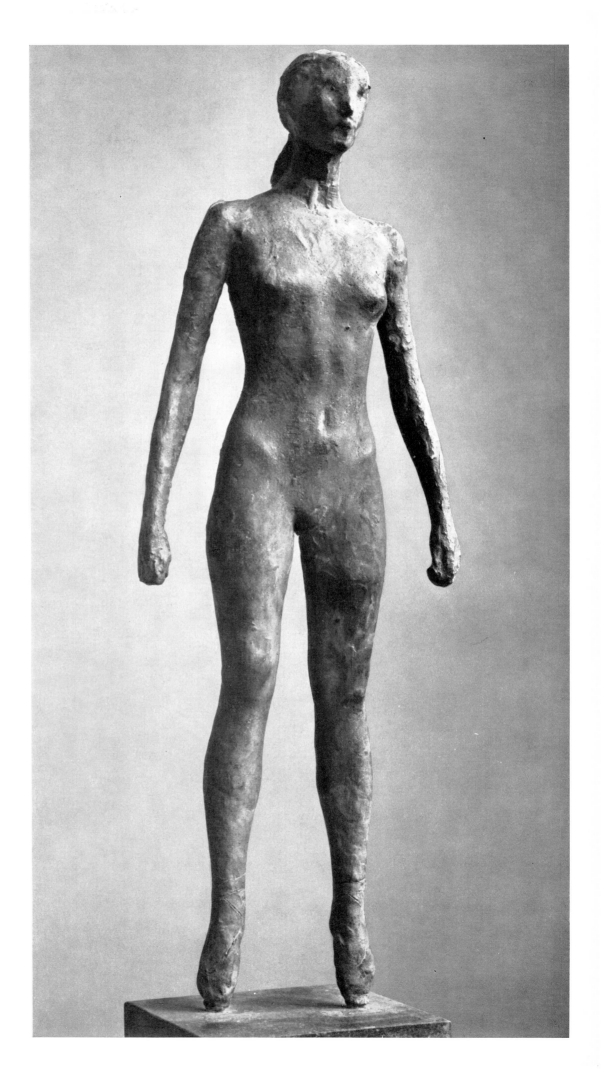

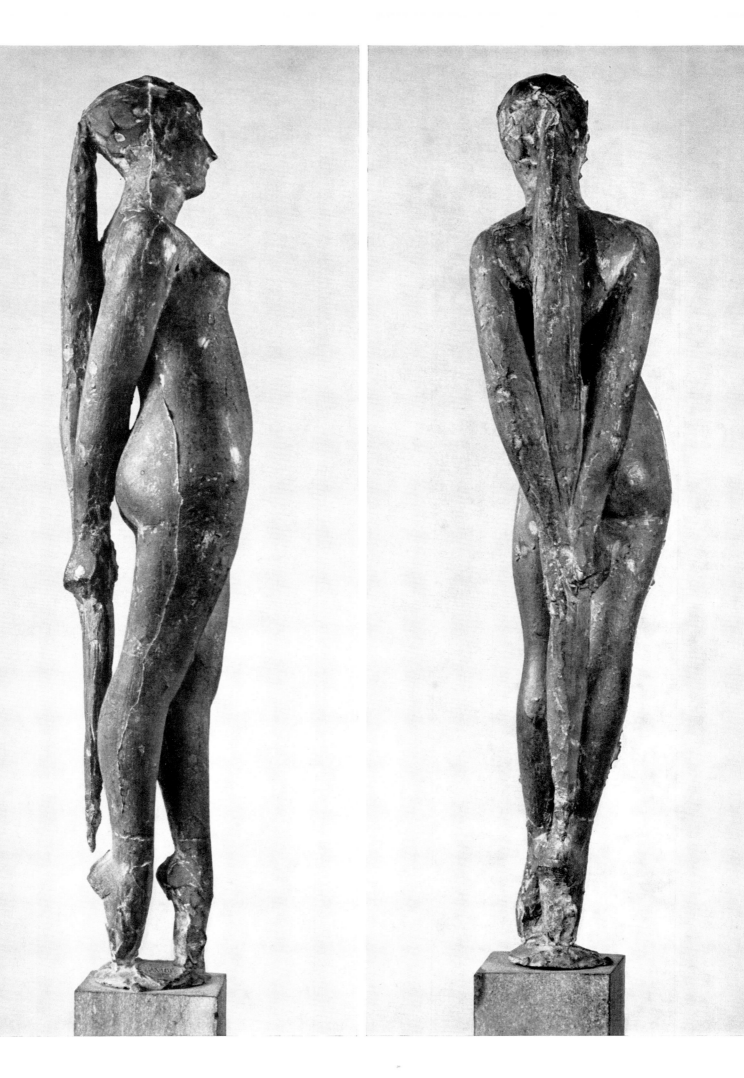

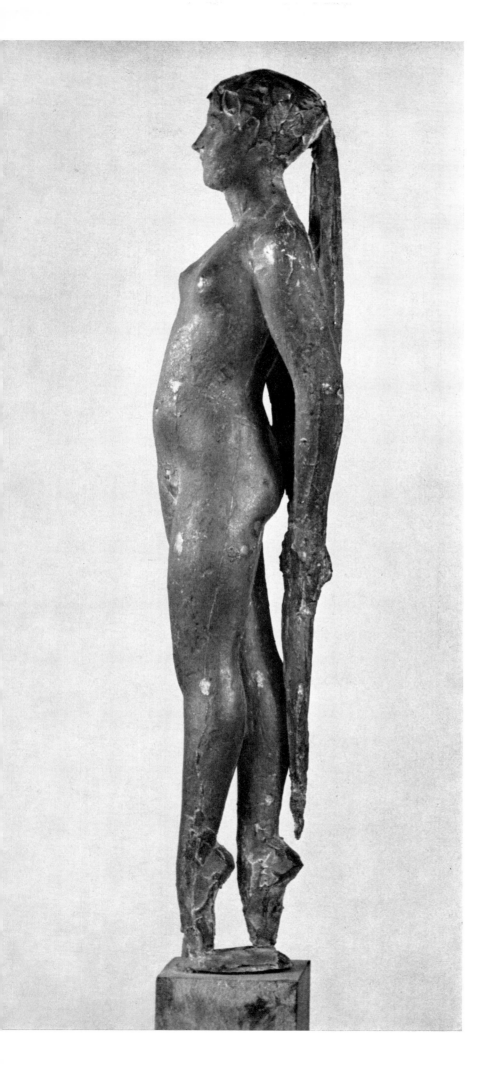

81

Dance Step, 1954
shown in three different views
Bronze, h. 20¹/₂″
Coll. Dr. Degenhart, Munich

Dance Step, 1956
Bronze, h. 27$^{1}/_{2}$''
Coll. Pio Manzoni, Bergamo

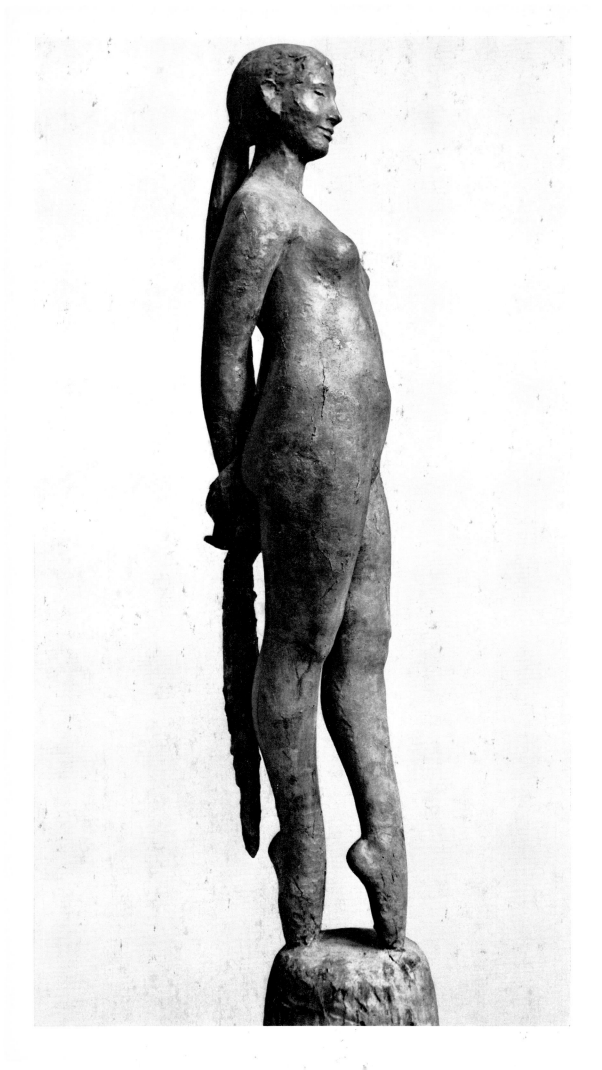

Dance Step, 1954
Bronze, h. 6′10⅝″
Private coll., Salzburg

84
Dance Step, 1954
Backview of plate 83

85
Dance Step, 1954
Detail of plate 86

86
Dance Step, 1954
Bronze, h. 7′2⅝″
Städtische Kunsthalle, Mannheim

Dancer, 1956
Bronze, h. 27$\frac{1}{2}$"
Coll. Erika Brausen, London

88

Dance Step, 1955
Bronze, h. 8'6³/₈"
Coll. Michael Behrens, London

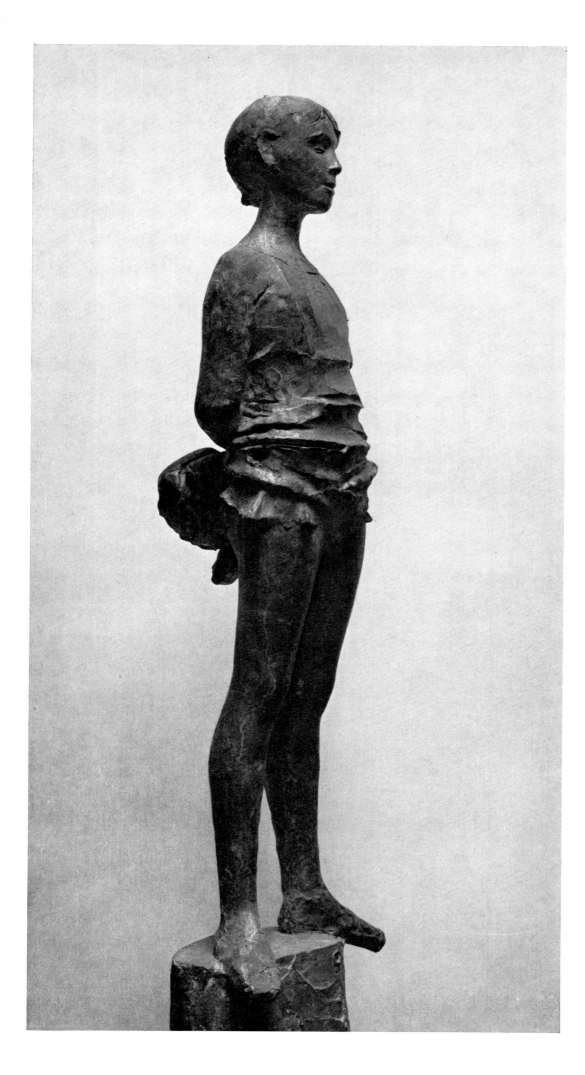

Ice Skater, 1957
Bronze, h. 4'7¹/₈''
Coll. Laing, Toronto

90

Dancer, 1957
Bronze, h. 25⁵/₈''
Coll. Pezzotta, Bergamo

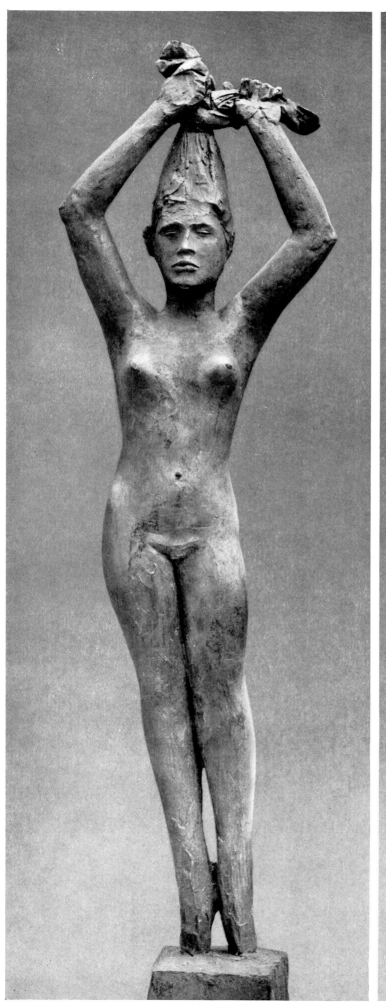

91

Girl Playing, 1956
Bronze, l. 25⅝"
Coll. Hodin, London

92

Mother and Child, 1956
Bronze, h. c. 15"
Private collection

93
Mother and Child, 1956
Bronze, h. c. 15″
Private coll., Paris

94
Mother and Child
Bronze, h. 15³/₄″
Coll. Bassetti, Milan

95

Ice Skater, 1957
Bronze, h. 7'2⅝"
Owned by the City of Antwerp

96

Ice Skater, 1957
Detail of plate 95

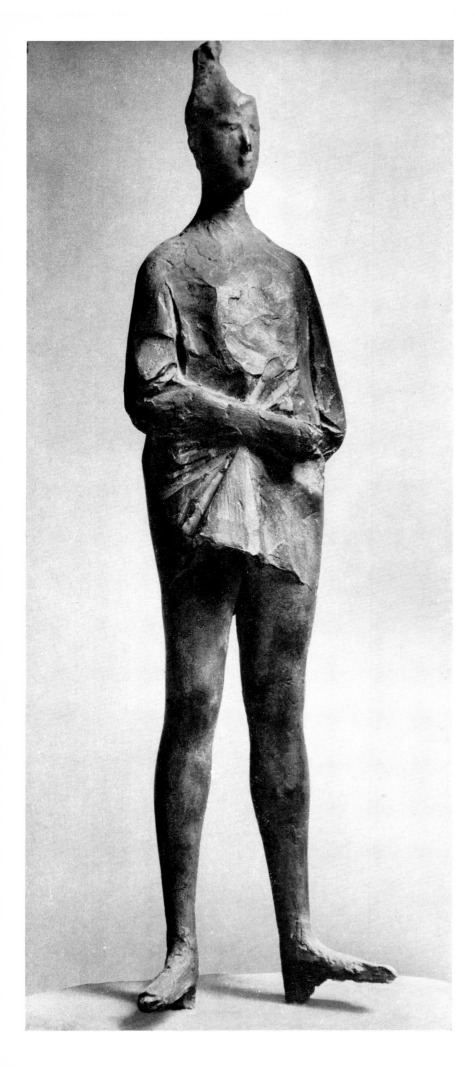

Ice Skater, 1957
Bronze, h. 25⅝"
Coll. A. Frumkin, Chicago

98

Bust of Inge, 1958
Bronze, h. 31½"
Private coll., Norway

99

Bust of Inge, 1956
Bronze, h. 28$^{3}/_{8}$''
Coll. John Schulte, New York

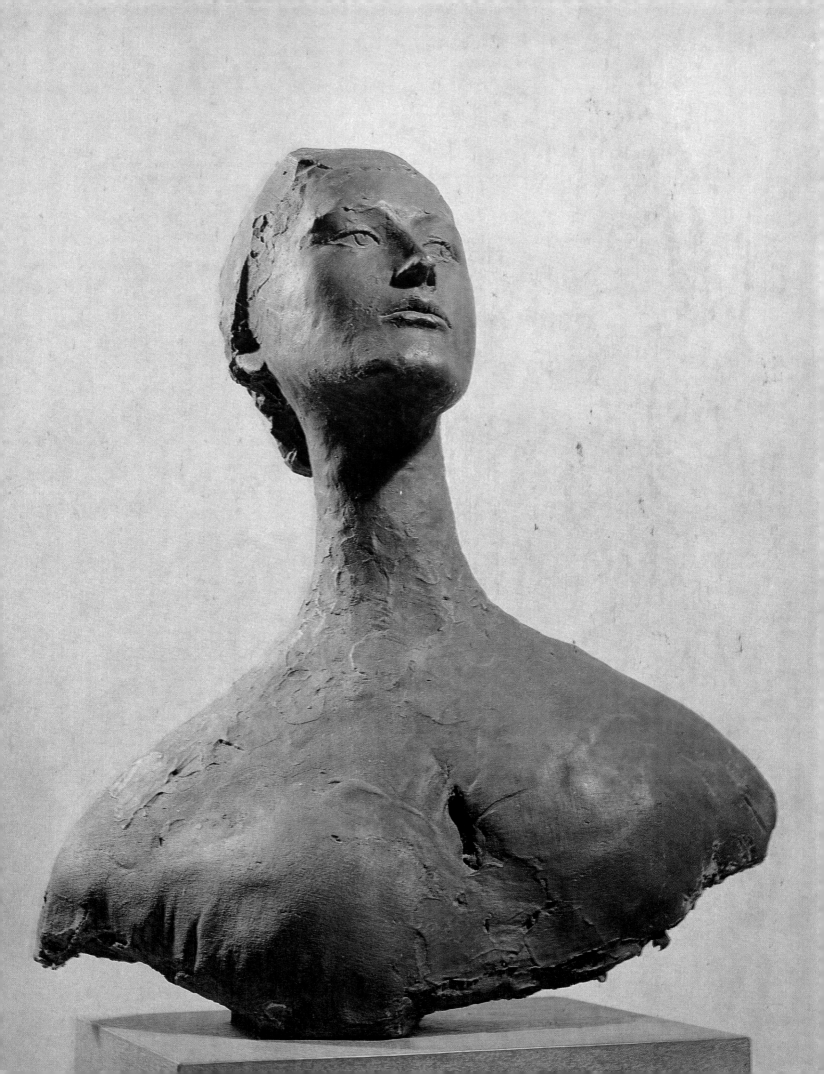

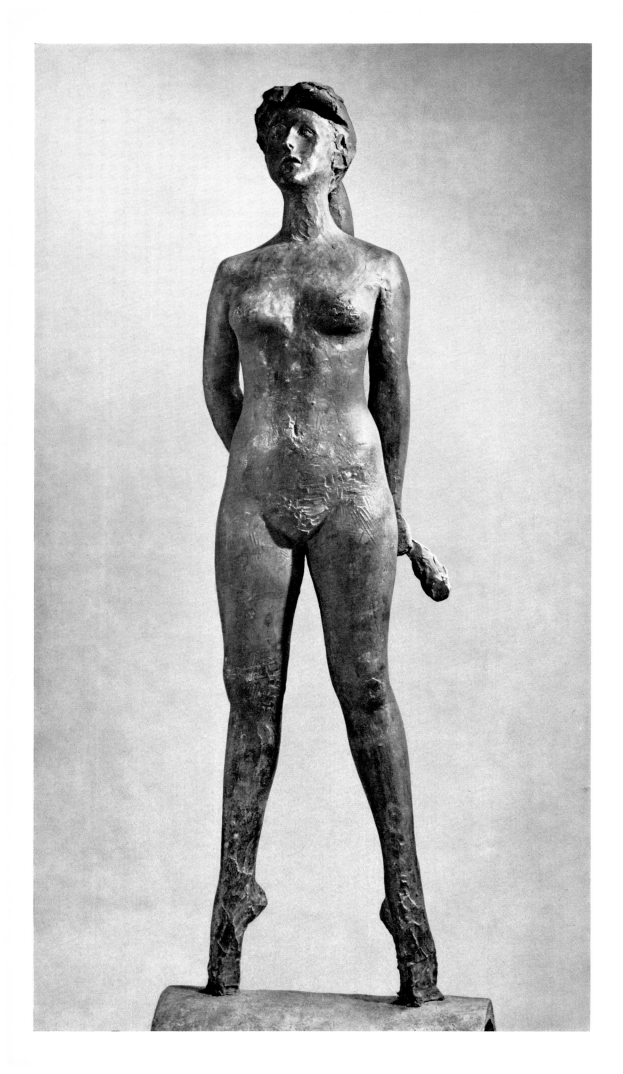

Dance Step, 1956
Bronze, h. 7'2⅝"
Coll. Morandi, Milan

101
Dance Step, 1956
Backview of plate 100

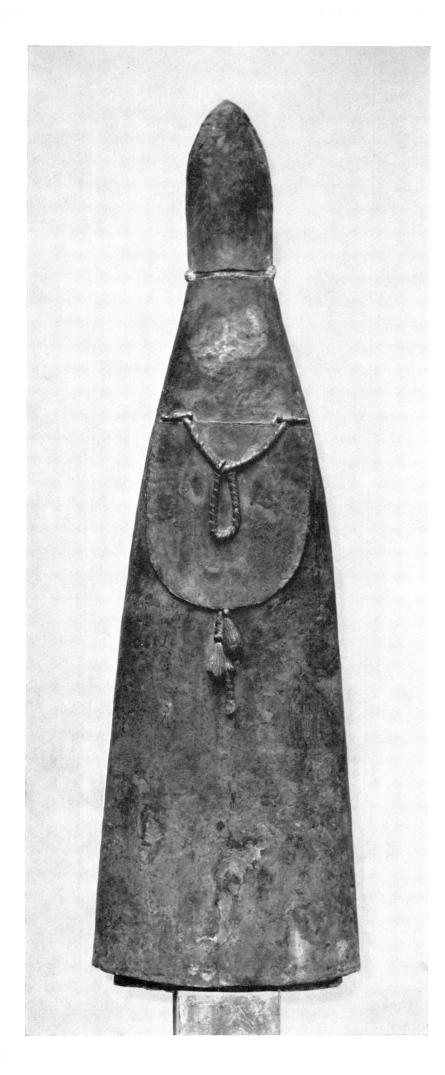

102
Backview of a Cardinal, 1958
Bronze, h. 5′3″
Private coll., New York

103

Cardinal, 1959
shown before the Arcades of
Salzburg Cathedral during
the Manzù Exhibition of 1960
Bronze, h. 10′10″

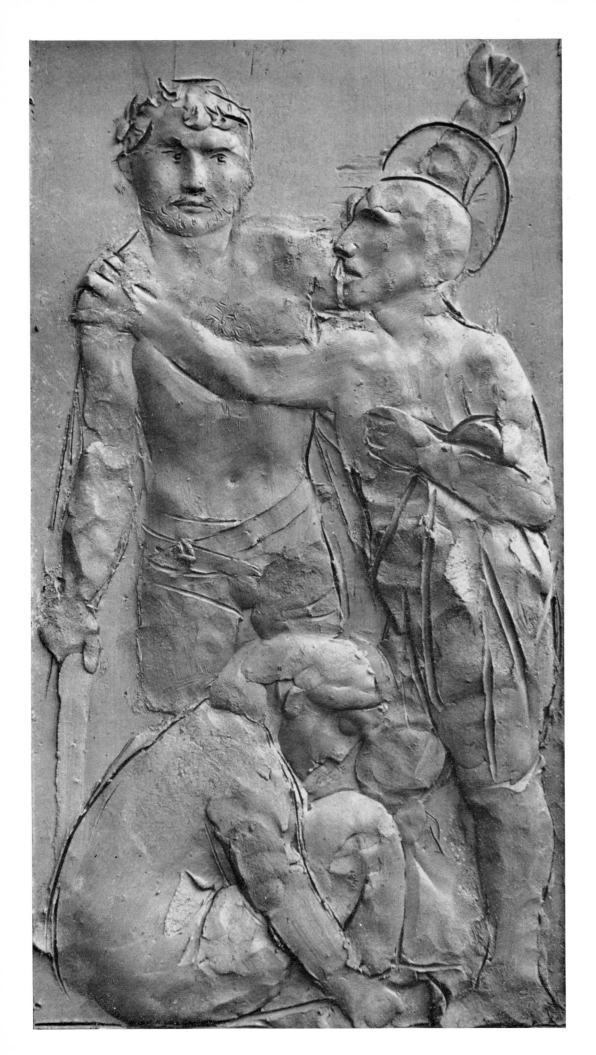

104

**Study for the Relief
of Saint Severin for the Door
of Salzburg Cathedral, 1958**
Detail of a relief in two sections
Bronze, 16³/₄×8⁵/₈″
Coll. Joseph Hirshhorn,
New York

**The Central Door of
Salzburg Cathedral, 1957**
Second Model
Bronze, 36¹/₄ × 18¹/₂″
Coll. Joseph Hirshhorn, New York

**The Door of Love,
Salzburg Cathedral, 1958**
Detail of the inner side, bronze

107

The Door of Love, 1958
Front view
Bronze, 14′3″ × 7′9″

108

Saint Martin, 1958
Relief, upper left part
of the Door for the
Cathedral, Salzburg

Saint Severin, 1958
Relief, upper right part
of the Door for the
Cathedral, Salzburg

First Study for the Broody Hen, 1958
Bronze, 10¹/₄ × 10¹/₄″
Subsequently destroyed by the artist

**Saint Notburga and the Beheading
of the Blessed Engelbert Kolland, 1958**
beneath them the symbolic animals:
Hen and Raven
Relief, lower left part of the Door for the
Cathedral, Salzburg

112
Study for the Dove, 1958
Bronze, 11×10⅝″
Coll. Joseph Hirshhorn, New York

113
Saint Konrad and Saint Francis of Assisi, 1958
beneath them the symbolic animals:
Dove and Pelican
Relief, lower right part of the Door for the
Cathedral, Salzburg

114

Key for the Door of Salzburg Cathedral
Enlarged Model
Bronze, h. 7′2⅝″
Private coll., London

115

Doorknob for the Door of Salzburg Cathedral
Grapevine and Wheatsheaf, Eucharistic Symbols
Bronze

Figure-study for the Door of Salzburg Cathedral
Not used in the final version
Bronze, $28^3/_4 \times 20^1/_2''$
Owned by the artist

**Third Project for the
Door of Saint Peter's
in the Vatican, 1949**
Bronze, h. 29¹/₈''
Owned by the artist

118

**The Door of Death
of Saint Peter's Basilica
in the Vatican, 1964**
Bronze, 25×12'

The Death of the Virgin, 1962
Study for the Relief in the
upper left part
Bronze, 33⁷/₈ × 17″
Paul Rosenberg Gallery,
New York

120

The Death of Christ, 1962
Study for the Relief in the
upper right part
Bronze, 29⁷/₈×15″

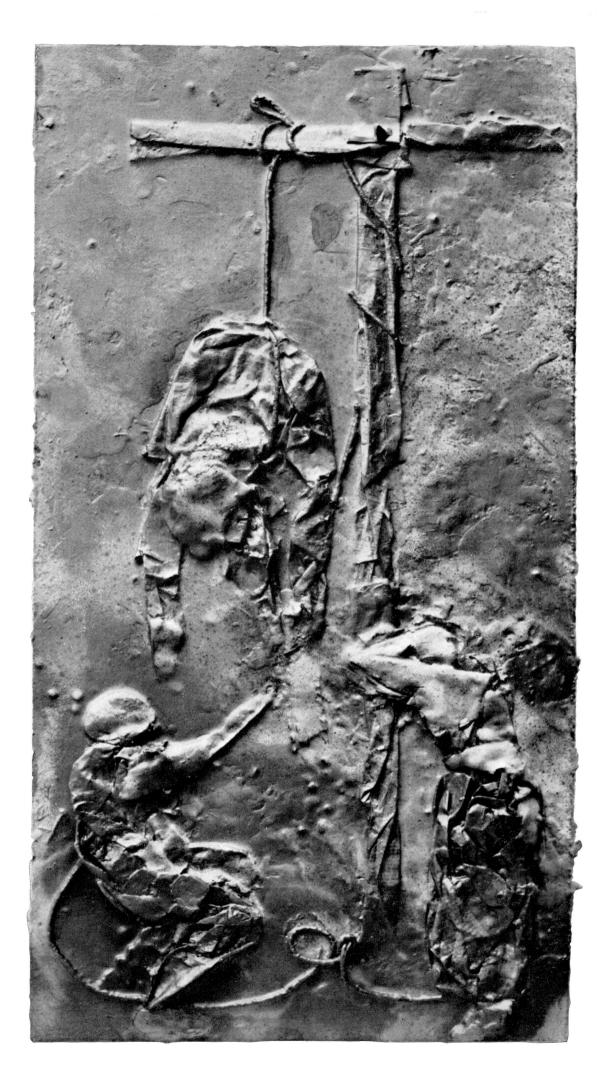

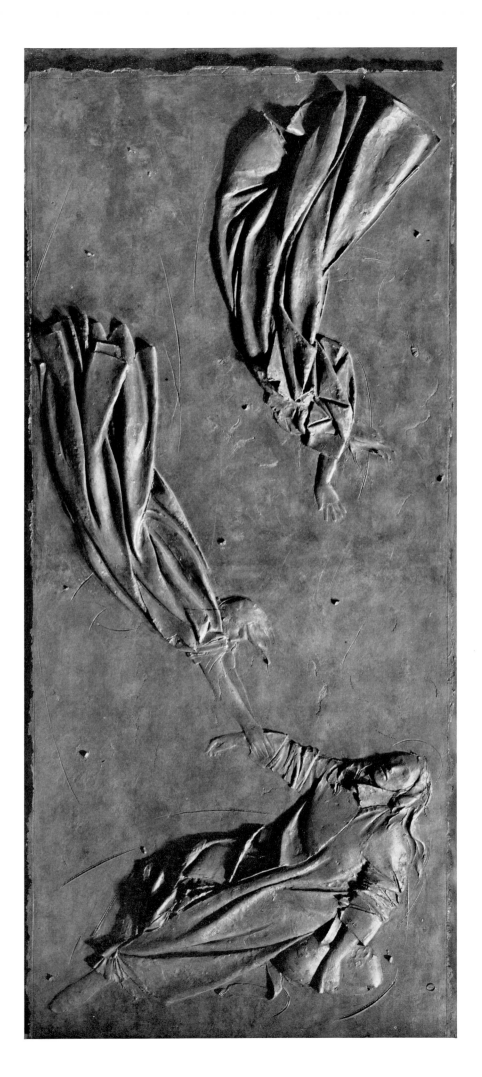

121

The Death of the Virgin, 1964
Relief in the upper part of the
left wing of the Vatican door
Bronze, 9′10″ × 4′1¼″

On the following pages:

123

**Reliefs in the lower part
of the left wing of the Vatican door, 1964**
The Death of Abel
The Death of Saint Joseph
Death Through Violence
The Death of John XXIII
Bronze, each relief c. 35½ × 25½″

122

The Death of Christ, 1964
Relief in the upper part of the
right wing of the Vatican door
Bronze, 9'10" × 4'1¼"

124

**Reliefs in the lower part
of the right wing of the Vatican door, 1964**
The Death of Saint Stephen
The Death of Gregory VII
Death in Space
Death on Earth
Bronze, each relief c. 35½" × 25½"

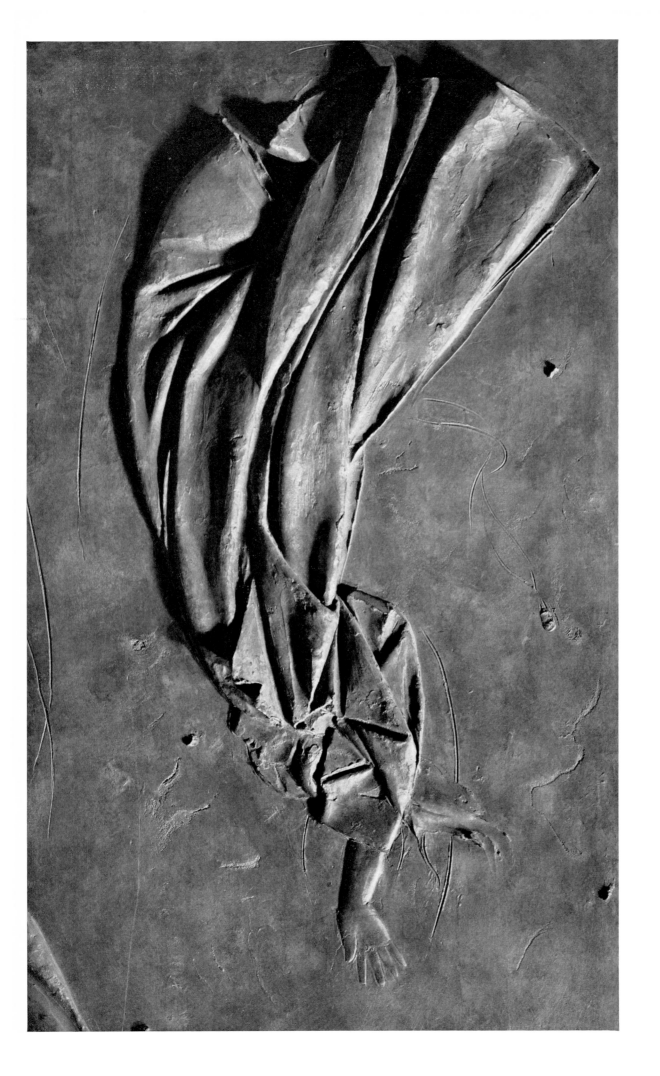

125

Downsweeping Angel, 1964
Detail of the Relief "The Death of the Virgin"

126

The Dying Virgin, 1964
Detail of the Relief "The Death of the Virgin"

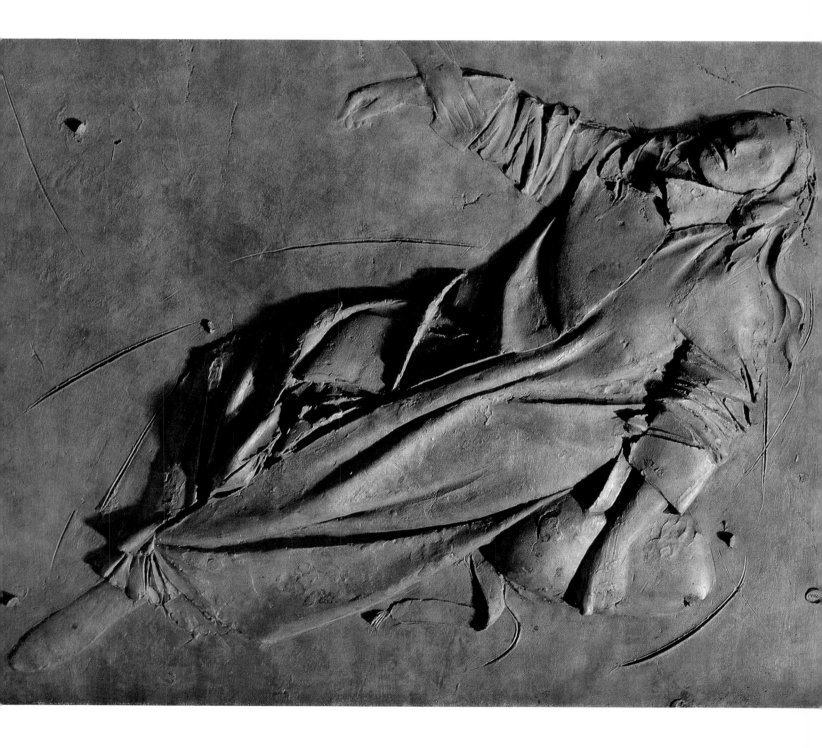

The Animals on the Door of Death

Hedgehog
Owl
Turtle with Snake
Dead Bird
Raven

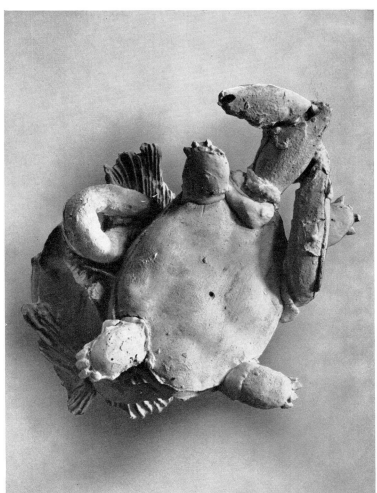
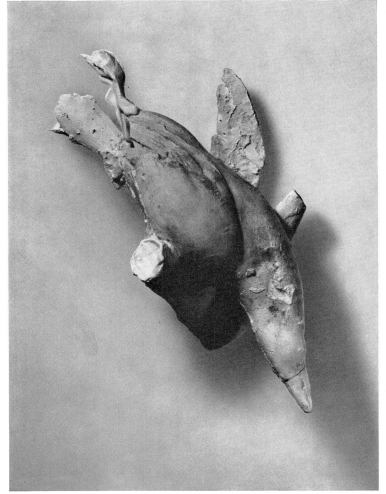

129

Study for the Relief "Death in Space", 1963
Bronze, 36¼×25⅛″
(Photographed from the clay model)
Coll. Ponti-Loren, Rome

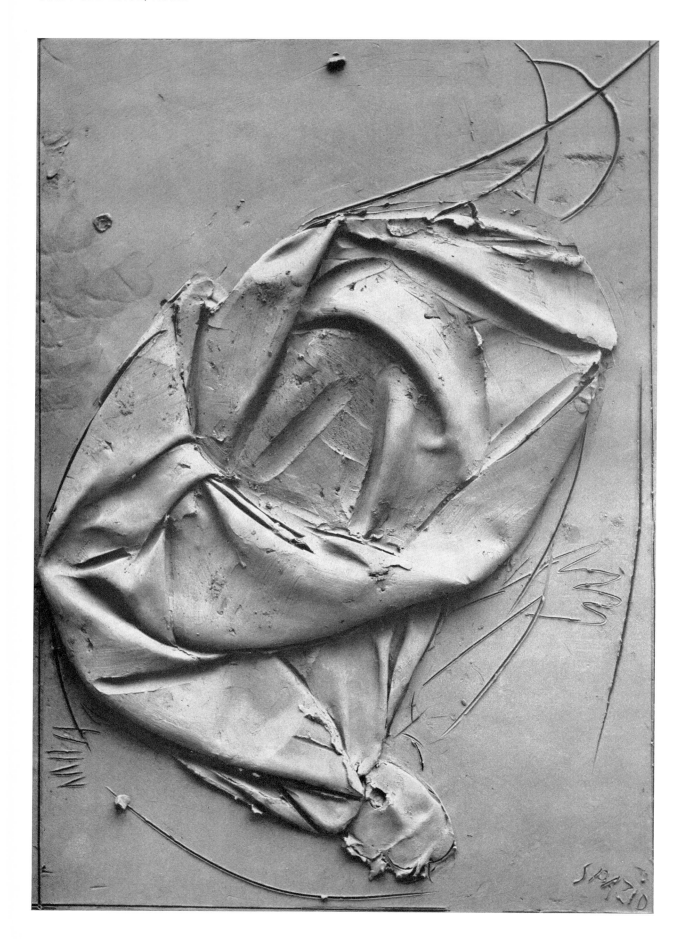

**Detail of a Study for the Relief
"The Death of Abraham", 1961**
This project was later eliminated
Bronze, 36⁵/₈✕24³/₄"
Owned by a Norwegian Museum

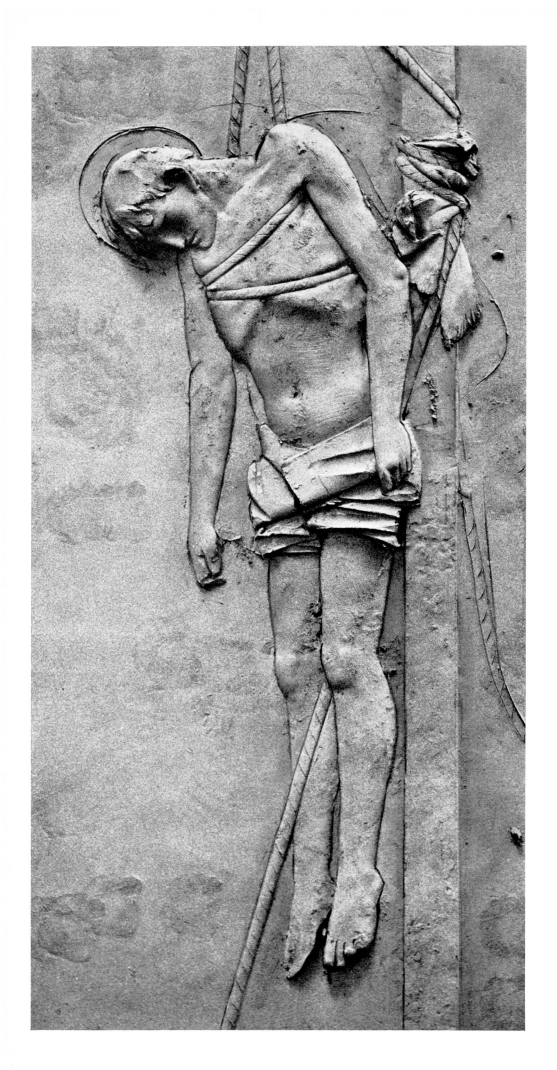

131

**Detail of a Study for
"The Death of Christ", 1963**
Size of the entire clay relief
9'10" × 4'1¼"

132

**Study for the Relief
"The Death of John XXIII", 1963**
Bronze, 38⅛ × 26"
(Photographed from the clay model)
Coll. Ponti-Loren, Rome

On the following pages:

133

**Study for the Relief
"Death Through Violence", 1963**
Bronze, 35⅞ × 24"
(Photographed from the clay model)

134

**Study for the Relief
"Death on Earth", 1963**
Bronze, 35⅞ × 24"
(Photographed from the clay model)

135

Inauguration of the Second Vatican Council, 1964
Relief-frieze on the inner side of the Door of Death
Bronze, c. 27$^{1}/_{2}$×12′

Below: Details from the frieze

Portrait Bust of Pope John XXIII (detail), 1963
Bronze, h. 36¼″
Vatican Collection

Head of Pope John XXIII, 1963
Bronze, h. 10¹/₄″
Coll. Monsignor Capovilla, Vatican

Bust of Inge, 1957
Bronze, h. 23⅝"
Coll. Herbert Mayer, New York

Bust of Inge, 1956
Bronze, h. 18⁷/₈″
Coll. Laing, Toronto

Bust of Inge, 1956
Bronze, h. 28³/₈″

Dancer (detail), 1957
Bronze, h. 7'2⅝"
Coll. Herbert Mayer, New York

Painter and Model, 1958
Bronze, h. 27$^{1}/_{2}$''
Coll. Pio Manzoni, Bergamo

143

Large Head of Inge, 1957
Bronze, h. 18⁷/₈″
Coll. Inge Schabel, Munich

Head of Inge, 1957
Bronze, h. 9⁷/₈″
Coll. Herbert Mayer, World House Galleries,
New York

145

Ice Skater, 1960
Bronze, h. 5'1"
Coll. Erika Brausen, London

146
Ice Skater, 1959
Bronze, h. c. 5'3"
Coll. Laing, Toronto

Head of Michael Park, 1964
Bronze, h. 11″
(Photographed from the clay model)
Owned by the artist

Bust of Inge (detail), 1961
Bronze, h. 17³/₄″
Private coll., Tokyo

149
Dance Step, 1956
Bronze, h. 33½″
Private coll., London

150
Dance Step, 1958
Bronze, h. 27½″
Private coll., Toronto

Dance Step, 1958
Detail of plate 150

Painter and Model
Bronze, h. 27¹/₂″
Coll. John Huston, Ireland

Ice Skater, 1959
Bronze, h. 5′1″
Coll. Campilli, Rome

154

Lovers, 1962
Bronze, l. c. 11³/₄″
(Photographed from the plaster model)
Coll. Yamasaki, Detroit

155

Study for a Couple of Lovers, 1965
Clay, l. 23⁵/₈"
Owned by the artist

156

Painter and Model, 1961
Bronze, h. c. 30³/₄″
Coll. Tazzoli, Turin

Painter and Model, 1960
Bronze, h. c. 17³/₄″
Coll. Erika Brausen, London

Bust of Inge, 1960
Bronze, h. 21$^{1}/_{4}$″
Coll. Inge Schabel, Munich

Head of Sonja, 1957
Bronze, h. $9^{1}/_{2}''$
Private coll., Munich

Portrait of Alice Rewald, 1961
Terracotta, h. 7⁷/₈″
Coll. John Rewald, New York

Head of Inge, 1956
Bronze, h. 10¹/₄″
Coll. Erika Brausen, London

Ballerina, 1962
Bronze, h. 20$^{1}/_{8}$''
Private coll., Tokyo

163

Ballerina, 1962
Bronze, h. 12⁵/₈″
Coll. Inge Schabel, Munich

Chair with Fruit, 1960
Gilded bronze, h. 39$^3/_8$″
Owned by the artist

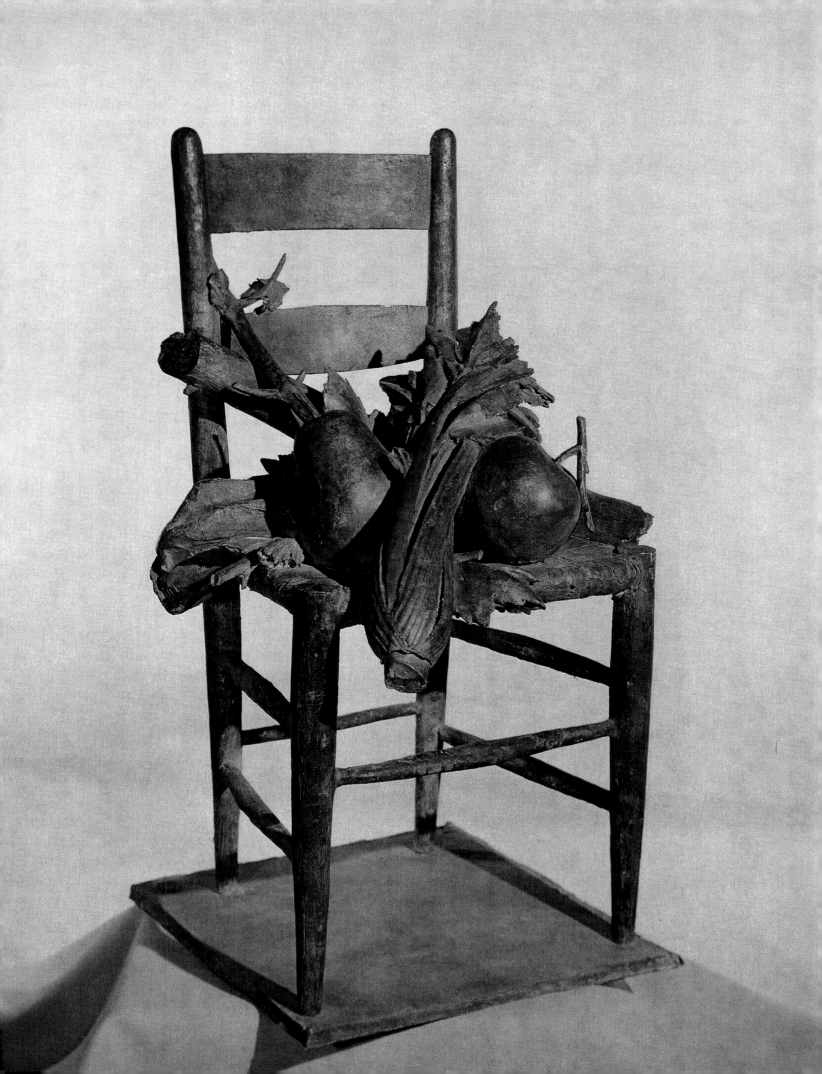

Bust of Sonja, 1962
Detail of plate 166

166
Bust of Sonja, 1962
Bronze, h. 26³/₈″
Coll. Pio Manzoni, Milan

Striptease, 1964
Bronze, h. 23¹/₄″
Paul Rosenberg Gallery, New Y

Ice Skater, 1960
Ebony, h. 6'2¾"
Coll. Agnelli, Turin

169

Faun and Nymph I, 1962
Sketch for a Fountain for McGregor University, Detroit
Bronze, l. c. 11³/₄″
Owned by the artist

170

Faun and Nymph II, 1962
Sketch for a Fountain for McGregor University, Detroit
Bronze, l. c. 11³/₄″
Owned by the artist

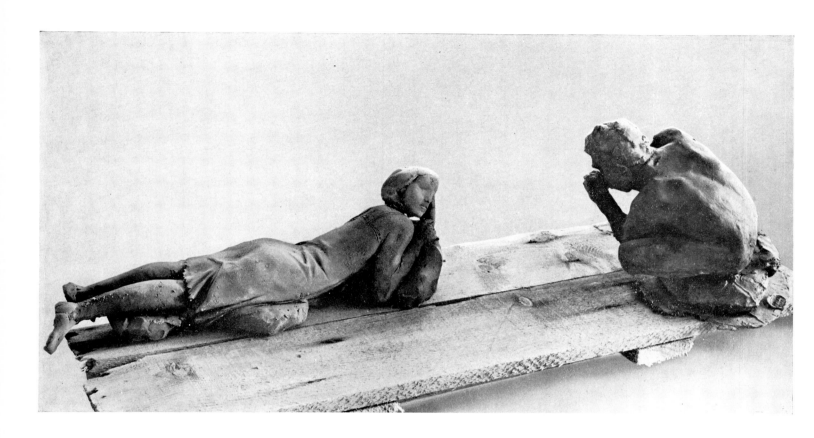

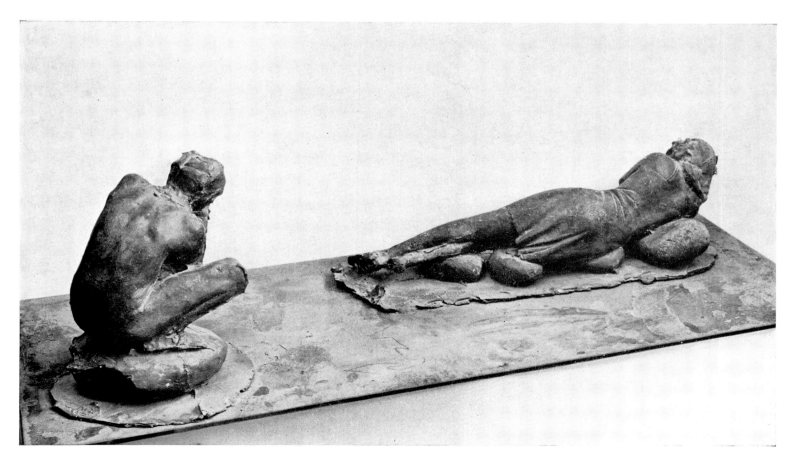

171

Young Girl, 1965
Bronze, h. 35''
Coll. Pio Manzoni, Bergamo

172
Bust of Inge, 1965
Bronze, h. 27½"
Paul Rosenberg Gallery,
New York

173

**Bust of Signora
Silvana Mangano
de Laurentiis, 1965**
Bronze, h. 20⅛"
Coll. de Laurentiis, Rome

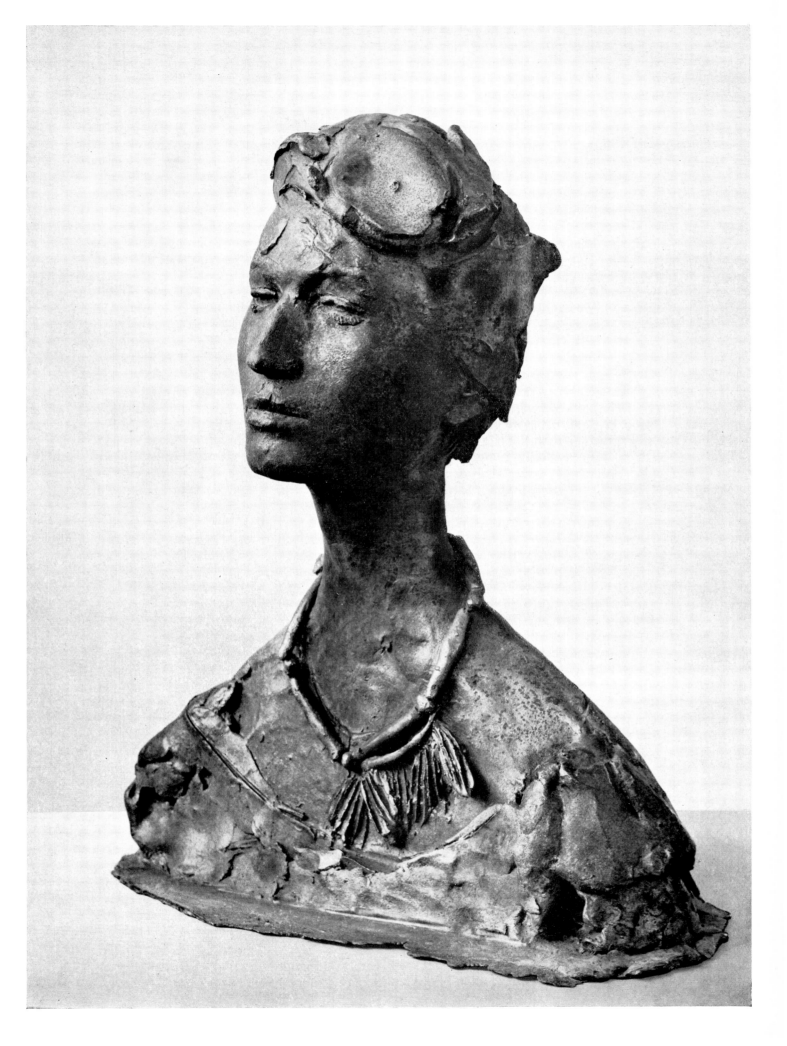

174

Dance Step, 1964
Bronze, h. 11'
Figure for the Fountain of the Detroit
Gas Company

Variations on a Theme, 1955—1965
Bas-reliefs, bronze, c. 70×50 cm.
Collection of the artist

After he had completed the doors of St Peter's, Manzù began work on a project which he had contemplated for many years. It was a development of his group of 1939, 'Cristo nella nostra umanità', and he gave the new series the title 'Variations on a Theme'. In it he returned to motifs on which he had first worked a quarter of a century ago as well as developing some completely new compositions. The continual obsession with the subject of self-sacrifice — the Vatican doors were, after all, also concerned with that subject — did not, however, in the least harm his spontaneity. Often flung casually onto an unframed rectangle with irregular edges which resemble handmade paper, these representations combine a graphic and even at times sketchy technique with masterly modelling. As a result of his varied treatment of the flat areas, these reliefs contain penetrating proof of Manzù's understanding of human suffering and of resignation and brutality. Accompanying his compassion are the recurring familiar figures of earlier works: the mourning women, the fettered and hanged partisans, the indifferent cardinals and the cynical soldiers. Manzù, true to himself as always, once again combined typical directness of expression with an extraordinary intensity of feeling.
Seven of these recently completed 'Variations on a Theme' are reproduced on the following pages.

BIOGRAPHICAL NOTES

BIBLIOGRAPHY

WORKS IN PUBLIC PLACES

WORKS OWNED BY MUSEUMS

SYSTEMATIC TABLES

The following systematic tables do not pretend to be complete. Carlo Ludovico Ragghianti in his monograph on Manzù, published in Milan in 1957 by Edizioni del Milione, had already labelled the systematic section as contributions. He was forced to do so because the artist lacked any type of bibliographic register and did dot know the final destination of his works.

I was therefore obliged to rely on the above-mentioned monograph, particularly for the period up to 1956. Information about subsequent years could be obtained from the Biblioteca dell'Istituto di Archeologia e Storia dell'Arte in the library of the Galleria Nazionale d'Arte Moderna and in the Biblioteca Hertziana. The editing of the various tables was based exclusively on chronological order.

Walter Zettl, Rome.

BIBLIOGRAPHY

A. Contributions by Giacomo Manzù

1. 'Dove va l'arte italiana?' In DOMUS, Milan, February 1937. Answer to a referendum.

2. 'Artisti italiani: Giacomo Manzù.' In IL FRONTE-SPIZIO, Florence, May 1937, No. 5, pp. I—VIII. This number is dedicated to Manzù; 10 of his sculptures and 12 of his drawings are reproduced. Autobiographical notes.

3. 'La Disciplina dell'Arte.' In PININFARINA, Turin 1964, No. 5, pp. 33—37.

B. Books illustrated by Giacomo Manzù, and folders of his graphic works

4. Piero Bargellini. ARCHITETTURA. Il Frontespizio, Florence 1934.

5. Nicola Lisi. PAESE DELL'ANIMA. Il Frontespizio, Florence 1934. With 20 vignettes.

6. Piero Bargellini. DAVIDE. Morcelliana, Brescia 1936. With 17 vignettes.

7. Arnaldo Beccaria. ADAMO. Edizioni della Cometa, Rome 1941. With an original etching.

8. Jacopone da Todi. LE LAUDI. Uomo, Milan 1945. With 8 plates.

9. IL NOVELLINO. Conchiglia, Milan 1947. With 30 plates.

10. Virgilio. LE GEORGICHE. Libreria Ulrico Hoepli, Milan 1947. Folder with 20 original etchings in an edition of 150 copies.

11. GEORGICA. Istituto Italiano d'Arti Grafiche, Bergamo 1948. Folder with etched studies in an edition of 21 copies.

12. Marta Vio. POESIA 1. DIALOGHI COL POETA. Schwarz Editore, Milan 1953. With 4 drawings.

13. Nicola Lisi. LA VIA DELLA CROCE. Fratelli Fabbri Editori, Milan 1954. With 8 reproductions.

14. Salvatore Quasimodo. IL FALSO E VERO VERDE. Schwarz Editore, Milan 1954. Numbered edition of 193 copies with 7 original lithographs and 6 etchings.

15. Loris Capovilla. GIOVANNI XXIII. Tipografia Poliglotta Vaticana, 1961. With 2 portrait sketches, one of them on the binding.

C. Monographs and introductions to the works of Giacomo Manzù

16. Giovanni Scheiwiller. MANZÙ. Libreria Ulrico Hoepli, Milan 1932. 12 pages of text and 10 plates.

17. Gianni Testori. MANZÙ, ERBE. Edizioni di Pattuglia 1. Forli 1942. Introduction: pp. 9—12, 15 plates of plant pictures.

18. Mario De Micheli. MANZÙ. Quaderni del Disegno Contemporaneo 2, Edizione di 'Corrente', Milan 1942. Preface: 6 pages, 24 reproductions and 1 coloured plate.

19. Nino Bertocchi. MANZÙ. Gruppo Editoriale Domus SA, Milan 1942. pp. I—VII text, 35 reproductions.

20. Ibid. 1943. pp. 5—17 text, 35 photographs and 1 original etching in an edition of 50 copies.

21. Bruno Calzaferri. VALORI UMANI E RELIGIOSI NELLA 'GRANDE PIETÀ' DI GIACOMO MANZÙ PER UN MONUMENTO PAPALE. Edizione della Conchiglia, Milan 1943. Bibliophile edition of 100 numbered copies regarding a design by Manzù for a papal memorial. Text: 5 pages, 6 plates and 1 reproduction in the text.

22. Luigi Bartolini. GIACOMO MANZÙ. Edizioni d'Arte Delfino 10. Edizioni Delfino, Rovereto 1944. Text: pp. 7—25, 32 plates.

23. Aligi Sassù. PASSIO CHRISTI, BASSORILIEVI DI MANZÙ. 'All'Insegna del Pesce d'Oro', Serie illustrata N. 32. Milan 1945. Introduction: 4 pages, 11 illustrations.

24. Beniamino Joppolo. GIACOMO MANZÙ. Arte Moderna Italiana N. 46, ed. Giovanni Scheiwiller, Serie B — Scultori N. 9. Ulrico Hoepli Editore, Milan 1946. Introduction: pp. 5—10, Biography: pp. 11—12, Bibliography: pp. 13—22, 32 plates.

25. Giulio Carlo Argan. MANZÙ, DISEGNI. Istituto Italiano d'Arti Grafiche, Bergamo 1948. Text: 8 pages, 28 reproductions and 1 photograph. Numbered edition of 1000 copies.

26. Anna Pacchioni. GIACOMO MANZÙ. Edizioni del Milione, Milan 1948. Preface by Lionello Venturi: pp. 7—9, Text: pp. 13—23, Biography: pp. 25—29, Bibliography: pp. 30—36, Exhibitions: p. 37, Catalogue of works: pp. 38—41, 80 plates, 8 reproductions in the text.

27. MANZÙ. IL BOZZETTO PER LE PORTE DI SAN PIETRO IN VATICANO. Secondo Concorso Roma 1949. Instituto Grafico Tiberino, Rome. (Design for the portals of St Peter's, 2nd competition.) Text: pp. 7—10, 14 plates.

28. Eduard Hüttinger. GIACOMO MANZÙ. Künstler unserer Zeit, Band II. Bodensee-Verlag, Amriswil 1956. Introduction: pp. 5—16, Biography: p. 17, Bibliography: pp. 18—21, 24 reproductions.

29. Carlo Ludovico Ragghianti. GIACOMO MANZÙ, SCULTORE. Edizioni del Milione, Milan 1957. Meetings with Manzù: pp. 5—41, Exhibitions: p. 43, Bibliography: pp. 44—65, Catalogue of works: pp. 66—72, 119 plates, one of them in the text and 1 photograph of the artist.

30. Bernhard Degenhart. GIACOMO MANZÙ, MÄDCHEN UND FRAUEN, 45 drawings, choice and postscript by Bernhard Degenhart. R. Piper & Co Verlag, Munich 1958. Postscript: pp. 49—57.

31. Franz Fuhrmann. GIACOMO MANZÙ, ENTWÜRFE ZUM SALZBURGER DOMTOR 1955/58. Verlag Galerie Welz, Salzburg 1958. Introduction: 9 pages, 45 reproductions.

32. Franz Fuhrmann. GIACOMO MANZÙ, DAS SALZBURGER DOMTOR, ENTWÜRFE UND AUSFÜHRUNGEN. Second expanded edition of ENTWÜRFE ZUM SALZBURGER DOMTOR (1958). Verlag Galerie Welz, Salzburg 1959. Introduction: 9 pages, 56 reproductions.

33. Robert d'Hooghe. GIACOMO MANZÙ. Verlag Galerie Welz, Salzburg 1960. Introduction: 9 pages; pictorial section 90 pages, with 6 pages intervening text; short biography.

34. Gabriele Mucchi. GIACOMO MANZÙ. Preface by Fritz Cremer. Exhibition of the Deutschen Akademie der Künste. Verlag der Kunst, Dresden 1960. Preface: pp. 5—6, Introduction: pp. 7—12, Biography: p. 13; 32 reproductions, 1 photograph of the artist.

35. Thomas Michels. DIE SALZBURGER DOMTORE. Verlag Galerie Welz, Salzburg 1960.

36. Cesare Brandi. QUARANTUN DISEGNI DI GIACOMO MANZÙ. Giulio Einaudi editore, Turin 1961. Folder of 41 facsimile prints of drawings in an edition of 1250 copies.

37. Bernhard Degenhart. GIACOMO MANZÙ, DONNE E FANCIULLE, 43 drawings, preface by Bernhard Degenhart. Translated by A. Chiusano. Biblioteca delle Silerchie LXV. Il Saggiatore, Milan 1961. Italian edition of No. 30, preface: pp. 7—13.

38. Lubor Kára. GIACOMO MANZÙ. Státni nakladatelstvi krásne literatury a uměni, Prague 1962. Text: pp. 7—57, Biography: p. 58; 80 reproductions, 16 of them in the text.

39. Cesare Brandi. LA PORTA DI SAN PIETRO — DAS PORTAL ZU ST PETER. Erker-Verlag, St Gallen 1964. Bilingual edition in Italian and German, 20 pages of text, 5 reproductions in the text, 42 plates.

40. Cesare Brandi. STUDI PER LA PORTA DI SAN PIETRO DI GIACOMO MANZÙ. Edizioni del Milione, Milan 1964. Sketches and variants, exhibited at XXXII Biennale in Vetnice, text: 23 pages, 27 reproductions.

D. Catalogues for exhibitions and documentation concerning films and opera

41. MOSTRA DI PITTURE, SCULTURE E DISEGNI DI MANZÙ. Preface by Piero Bargellini. 8 plates. Hôtel Milano-Selvino, Bergamo, 15—30 August 1933.

42. MOSTRA PERSONALE DI GIACOMO MANZÙ. Preface by Carlo Carrà. Galleria della Cometa, Rome, 18 March to 1 April 1937.

43. RENATO BIROLLI — GIACOMO MANZÙ. Preface by Nino Bertocchi. Galleria Genova, Genoa, 12—28 October 1938.

44. GIACOMO MANZÙ. Preface by Umbro Apollonio. Galleria d'Arte al Corso. Trieste, November to December 1941.

45. MOSTRA PERSONALE. Preface by Nino Bertocchi. Centro d'Azione per le Arti, Turin 1942.

46. MAFEI E MANZÙ. Preface by Alberto Moravia. Galleria dello Zodiaco, Rome 1943.

47. MANZÙ. Preface by Lionello Venturi. Palazzo Exreale, Gruppo L'Altano, Milan, March 1947.

48. GIACOMO MANZÙ, ESCULTURAS Y DIBUJOS. Preface by Nino Bertocchi. Instituto de Arte Moderno, Buenos Aires, November 1949.

49. GIACOMO MANZÙ. Introduction by Fortunato Bellonzi, pp. 25/26. VI. Quadriennale nazionale d'arte di Roma, Rome, December 1951 to April 1952.

50. GIACOMO MANZÙ, 36 DISEGNI. Preface by Alberto Rossi. Salone de La Stampa, Turin, April—May 1953.

51. GIACOMO MANZÙ. Preface by Eric Newton. The Hanover Gallery, London, May—June 1953.

52. GIACOMO MANZÙ, SKULPTUREN UND HANDZEICHNUNGEN. Preface by Ernst Köller. Galerie Welz Salzburg, Summer 1954.

53. MANZÙ. Preface by Guido Ballo. La Colonna, Milan, October 1954.

54. MANZÙ-SONDERAUSSTELLUNG IN DER JAHRESAUSSTELLUNG DES GRAZER KÜNSTLERHAUSES, December 1954 to January 1955. Preface by F. R. Oberhuber. Organization: Galerie Welz Salzburg.

55. MOSTRA DI LITOGRAFIE DI GIACOMO MANZÙ. Preface by Guido Ballo. Galleria d'arte Cosmé, Ferrara, March 1955.

56. MANZÙ. Preface by Bruno Grimschitz. Kunsthalle Bremen, 1955. Organization: Galerie Welz Salzburg.

57. MANZÙ. Preface by Bruno Grimschitz. Cologne, 1955. Organization: Galerie Welz Salzburg.

58. MANZÙ. Preface by Bruno Grimschitz. Neue Galerie der Stadt Linz, 1955. Organization: Galerie Welz Salzburg.

59. MANZÙ. Preface by Bruno Grimschitz. Museumspavillon Mirabell, Salzburg, 1955. Organization: Galerie Welz Salzburg.

60. GIACOMO MANZÙ. Preface by Bruno Grimschitz. Württembergischer Kunstverein, Stuttgart 1955. Organization: Galerie Welz Salzburg. Joint exhibition with Alberto Giacometti.

61. GIACOMO MANZÙ, BRONZESKULPTUREN, AQUARELLE, HANDZEICHNUNGEN, GRAPHIK. Preface by Bruno Grimschitz. Organized by the Österreichischen Kulturvereinigung im Österreichischen Museum für angewandte Kunst, Wien 1955. Organization: Galerie Welz Salzburg.

62. MANZÙ. Preface by Bruno Grimschitz. Centraal Museum, Utrecht, 24 November 1955 to 1 February 1956. Organization: Galerie Welz Salzburg.

63. GIACOMO MANZÙ, STUDIO PER UN RITRATTO. Preface by Carlo Ludovico Ragghianti. Exhibition of 70 drawings of the collection Arrigo Lampugnani, Milan. Palazzo Strozzi, Florence, February—March 1956.

64. GIACOMO MANZÙ. Introduction by Cesare Brandi, pp. 80—83. XXVIII Esposizione Biennale Internazionale d'Arte, Venice 1956.

65. MANZÙ E QUASIMODO. Per i partigiani di Valenza. Introduction by Renato Usiglio. Galleria d'Arte La Colonna, Milan, 17—30 April 1957.

66. MANZÙ. Introduction by Guido Ballo. Galleria del Girasole, Udine, 9—22 November 1957.

67. MANZÙ. First One-Man Exhibition in the United States, a Selection of Bronzes, Bas-Reliefs, Drawings. Introduction by John Rewald. World House Galleries, New York, 24 April to 18 May 1957.

68. MANZÙ. Introduction by C. Joshua Taylor. Allan Frumkin Gallery, Chicago 1958.

69. GIACOMO MANZÙ, ACQUEFORTI E LITOGRAFIE. Introduction by Guido Perocco. Preface by Giorgio Trentin. Comune di Venezia, Opera Bevilacqua La Masa, Venice, 4—20 May 1958.

70. GIACOMO MANZÙ. Contributions by Bernhard Degenhart and Carlo Ludovico Ragghianti. Haus der Kunst, Munich, 15 August to 4 October 1959. Organization: Galerie Welz Salzburg.

71. GIACOMO MANZÙ. Contributions by Bernhard Degenhart and Carlo Ludovico Ragghianti. Historisches Museum, Frankfurt am Main, 14 November 1959 to 3 January 1960. Organization: Galerie Welz Salzburg.

72. GIACOMO MANZÙ. SKULPTUREN, ZEICHNUNGEN. Introduction by Gabriele Mucchi, Preface by Helga Weißgärber. Nationalgalerie der Staatlichen Museen zu Berlin, 1960. Organization: Galerie Welz Salzburg.

73. MANZÙ. Introduction by Mario Miniaci. World House Galleries, New York, 5 April to 7 May 1960.

74. GIACOMO MANZÙ, SKULPTUREN, ZEICHNUN-GEN, GRAPHIK. Introduction by Cesare Brandi (German and Italian). Galerie 'im Erker', St Gallen, 9 April to 31 May 1960.

75. GIACOMO MANZÙ, VEISTOKSIA PIIRUSTUKSIA — SKULPTURER TECKNINGAR. Introduction by Carlo Ludovico Ragghianti (Finnish and Swedish). Finn-ländische Kunstakademie 'Ateneum', Helsinki, 14 April to 8 May 1960. Organization: Galerie Welz Salzburg.

76. GIACOMO MANZÙ. Contributions by Bernhard De-genhart and Carlo Ludovico Ragghianti. Organized by Galerie Welz in the Zwerglgarten, Salzburg, 15 June to 11 September 1960.

77. GIACOMO MANZÙ. SCULPTURE AND DRAWINGS. Introduction by Carlo Ludovico Ragghianti. Tate Gallery, London, 1 October to 6 November 1960. Organization: Galerie Welz Salzburg.

78. MANZÙ. Introduction by Luigi Carluccio. Galleria Galatea, Turin, 27 February to 20 March 1961.

79. MANZÙ — GUTTUSO. Introduction by Luigi Car-luccio. Galerie 'La Nuova Pesa', Rome, 30 March to 15 April 1961.

80. DISEGNI DI MANZÙ. Preface by Tino Simoncini (Sindaco von Bergamo). Palazzo della Pinacotecca Carrara, Bergamo, 15—30 September 1962.

81. DISEGNI DEGLI 'ANNI TRENTA' DI BIROLLI, GROSSO, MANZÙ, SASSÙ, TOMEA. Introduction by Renato Usiglio. Galleria 'L'Approdo', Turin, 25 January to 20 February 1964.

82. L'OPERA GRAFICA DI GIACOMO MANZÙ DAL 1929 AL 1964. Introduction by Carlo Ludovico Ragghianti: 'Fantasia e memoria nella grafica di Manzù'. Galerie 'La Nuova Pesa', Rome, November 1964. Università di Pisa — Istituto di storia dell'arte, Gabinetto disegni e stampe.

83. DRAWINGS BY GIACOMO MANZÙ. Galleria Odys-sia, New York, 10 November to 5 December 1964.

84. LA PORTA DI SAN PIETRO DI GIACOMO MANZÙ. Publication of the Ufficio Stampa Dino De Lauren-tiis Cinematografia Distribuzione S. p. A. concerning the documentary film of the same title. Director: Clauco Pellegrini, Text: Carlo Levi, Music: Goffredo Petrassi, 1964.

85. MANZÙ. Introduction by Luigi Carluccio. Galleria Galatea, Turin, 19 November 1964 to 5 January 1965.

86. GIACOMO MANZÙ. Hanover Gallery, London, 25 January to 26 February 1965.

87. GIACOMO MANZÙ, BILDER UND ZEICHNUNGEN. Galerie Gimpel, Zürich, 5 March to 7 April 1965.

88. OEDIPUS REX. Programme of the Teatro dell' Opera, Rome, for the performance of the scenic oratorio by Igor Stravinsky on 3 March 1965. Scen-ery and costumes by Giacomo Manzù.

89. DISEGNI E LITOGRAFIE DI MANZÙ. Galleria Ci-ranna, Milan, 6 May to 5 June 1965.

90. THE BRONZE RELIEFS FOR THE DOOR OF SAINT PETER'S. Paul Rosenberg & Co., New York, 6 De-cember 1965 to 29 January 1966.

91. DIE RELIEFS VON GIACOMO MANZÙ. Preface by Peter H. Feist. Galerie Welz Salzburg, Summer 1966

91a) GIACOMO MANZÙ. Gallery Cube, Tokyo, March 1966.

E. Reports in journals and important articles in news-papers

92. Gino Visentin. 'Manzù scultore'. LA VOCE DI BER-GAMO, Bergamo, 10 March 1930.

93. Agnoldomenico Pica. 'Manzù'. DOMUS, Milan, Fe-bruary 1932.

94. Eva Randi. 'Manzù'. ORPHEUS, Milan, February 1933.

95. Lamberto Vitali. 'Sculture di Giacomo Manzù'. DOMUS, Milan, February 1933.

96. Umbro Apollonio. 'Manzu'. LE ARTI PLASTICHE, Milan, 16 April 1933.

97. Giovanni Scheiwiller. 'Un primitivo: Giacomo Manzù'. CORRIERE PADANO, Ferrara, February 1934.

98. Raffaello Giolli. 'Manzù'. L'ITALIA LETTERARIA, Rome, 16 June 1934.

99. Sandro Bini. 'Lo scultore Giacomo Manzù'. ARTE CRISTIANA, Milan, May 1935.

100. Alfredo Schettini. 'Lo scultore Manzù e l'arte cri-stiana'. L'ECO DEL MONDO, Milan, 29 June 1935.

101. Geo Renato Crippa. 'Giacomo Manzù'. L'ORTO, Bologna, March—April 1936.

102. Raffaele De Grada, jr. 'Giacomo Manzù'. L'ORTO, Bologna, March—April 1936.

103. Giuseppe Pensabene. 'Sculture di Giacomo Manzù'. QUADRIVIO, Rome, 4 April 1937.

104. Gino Visentin. 'Giacomo Manzù'. L'ORTO, Bologna, April 1937.

105. Renato Birolli. 'Testimonianza su Giacomo Manzù'. CORRENTE DI VITA GIOVANILE, Milan, 15 April 1938.

106. Lamberto Vitali. 'Lo scultore Giacomo Manzù'. EMPORIUM, Bergamo, May 1938.

107. Aniceto de Massa. 'Giacomo Manzù'. LA NAZIONE, Florence, 2 June 1938.

108. Libero De Libero. 'Scultura di Giacomo Manzù'. IL BROLETTO, Como, June 1938.

109. Renzo Guaso. 'Visita a Manzù'. CORRENTE DI VITA GIOVANILE, Milan, 30 September 1938.

110. Umbro Apollonio. 'Giacomo Manzù'. IL VENTUNO, Venice, December 1938.

111. Umbro Apollonio. 'Giacomo Manzù'. IL POPOLO DEL FRIULI, Udine, 31 January 1939.

112. Cesare Brandi. 'Su alcuni giovani: Manzù'. LE ARTI, Rome, February—March 1939.

113. Giuseppe Ardinghi. 'Appunti sulla Quadriennale: Morandi e Manzù'. IL BARGELLO, Florence, 24 March 1939.

114. Nino Bertocchi. 'Giacomo Manzù'. CORRENTE DI VITA GIOVANILE, Milan, 31 March 1939.

115. Luigi Bartolini. 'Manzù alla Quadriennale'. CORRENTE DI VITA GIOVANILE, Milan, 31 March 1939.

116. Sandro Bini. 'I disegni di Manzù'. CORRENTE DI VITA GIOVANILE, Milan, 15 October 1939.

117. Renzo Guasco. 'Due momenti su Manzù'. CORRENTE DI VITA GIOVANILE, Milan, 19 November 1939.

118. Gino Visentin. 'Sacro e profano di Manzù'. STORIA DI IERI E DI OGGI, Rome, January 1940.

119. Enotrio Mastrolonardo. 'Artisti d'Oggi: Giacomo Manzù'. MERIDIANO DI ROMA, Rome, 21 April 1940.

120. Carlo Carrà. 'Manzù'. ALMANACCO 'TESORETTO', Milan 1940.

121. Nino Bertocchi. 'Manzù e la critica'. PRIMATO, Rome, 15 February 1941.

122. Cesare Brandi. 'Una Mostra di Manzù'. LE ARTI, Rome, February—March 1941.

123. Mario De Micheli. 'Nota su Manzù'. ARCHITRAVE, Bologna, 1 March 1941.

124. Nino Bertocchi. 'Il Davide di Manzù'. PRIMATO, Rome, 1 March 1942.

125. Aldo Bertini. 'Un'esposizione di Manzù'. EMPORIUM, Bergamo, July 1942.

126. Giuseppe Pagano Pogatschnig. 'Pagina di Manzù'. STILE, Milan, September 1942.

127. Nino Bertocchi. 'Giacomo Manzù'. DOMUS, Milan, October 1942.

128. Giulio Carlo Argan. 'Manzu'. BELTEMPO, ALMANACCO DELLE LETTERE E DELLE ARTI, Rome 1942.

129. M. di R. 'Timore per Giacomo Manzù'. MERIDIANO DI ROMA, Rome, 30 May 1943.

130. Luigi Bartolini. 'La scultura e lo scultore Manzù'. QUADRIVIO, Rome, 6 June 1943.

131. E. Maselli. 'Manzù e la scultura'. IL LAVORO FASCISTA, Rome, 13 June 1943.

132. Lamberto Vitali. 'Manzù'. WERK, Winterthur 1945.

133. Giorgio Mottana. 'Omaggio a Manzù'. IL SENTIMENTO, Como, September—October 1946.

134. Nino Bertocchi. 'Manzù padrone delle cose'. CRONACHE, Bologna, 22 March 1947.

135. Gillo Dorfles. 'Giacomo Manzù'. LA FIERA LETTERARIA, Rome, 27 March 1947.

136. Luigi Bartolini. '13 punti su Manzù'. ALFABETO, Rome, 15—30 April 1947.

137. Emilio Villa. 'L'ultima statua di Manzù'. ALFABETO, Rome, 15—30 April 1947.

138. Lionello Venturi. 'Manzù'. ALFABETO, Rome, 15—30 April 1947.

139. Garibaldo Marussi. 'Manzù, scultore pensoso'. PESCI ROSSI, Milan, April 1947.

140. Fortunato Bellonzi. 'Elogio di Manzù'. LA VOCE REPUBBLICANA, Rome, 8 May 1947.

141. Alberto Bragaglia. 'Difesa di Manzù'. IL BUONSENSO, Rome, 15 May 1947.

142. Libero De Libero. 'Manzù'. LA FIERA LETTERARIA, Rome, 15 May 1947.

143. Vincenzo Costantini. 'Manzù'. LE ARTI BELLE. Milan, May 1947.

144. Attilio Podestà. 'Riepilogo di Manzù'. EMPORIUM, Bergamo, May 1947.

145. Toti Scialoja. 'Ritratto di Signora di Manzù'. L'IMMAGINE, Rome, May 1947.

146. Luigi Carluccio. 'In cerca di Manzù'. AGORÀ, Turin, August 1947.

147. Emilio Lavagnino. 'Il concorso per le due nuove porte di bronzo a S. Pietro'. CAPITOLIUM, Rome, January—March 1948.

148. Ennio Francia. 'Le porte di S. Pietro'. IL POPOLO, Rome, 8 February 1948.

149. Marcello Piacentini. 'Per le nuove porte di San Pietro'. LA FIERA LETTERARIA, Rome, 13 February 1948.

150. Adriano Prandi. 'Sulla mostra dei bozzetti per le porte della Basilica Vaticana'. L'OSSERVATORE ROMANO, Città del Vaticano, 16—17 February 1948.

151. Virgilio Guzzi. 'Le porte di bronzo a San Pietro'. L'ILLUSTRAZIONE ITALIANA, Milan, 29 February 1948.

152. Francesco Muti. 'Orientamenti critici sulle porte di San Pietro'. L'OSSERVATORE ROMANO, Città del Vaticano, 20 February 1948.

153. Deoclecio Redig de Campos. 'Critica della critica, a proposito del concorso per le porte di S. Pietro'. IL QUOTIDIANO, Rome, 22 February 1948.

154. Giovanni Fallani. 'Le nuove porte di San Pietro'. ECCLESIA, Città del Vaticano, March 1948.

155. Alberico Sata. 'Alle labbra delle creature di Manzù respira l'alba della vita'. GIORNALE DEL POPOLO, Bergamo, 9 June 1948.

156. Luciano Pasqualini. 'Incontro con Giacomo Manzù'. IL SENTIERO DELL'ARTE, Pesaro, 15 June 1948.

157. Agnoldomenico Pica. 'Sculture di Manzù'. VERNICE, Trieste, June—July 1948.

158. Giuseppe Marchiori. 'Due scultori: Marini e Manzù'. ULISSE, Rome, July 1948.

159. Palma Bucarelli. 'Tendences actuelles de l'art en Italie'. ARTS, Paris, 3 September 1948.

160. Nino Bertocchi. 'Giacomo Manzù: Grande ritratto di signora'. (Introduction to a reproduction.) ARTE MEDITERRANEA, Florence, January — February 1949.

161. Cesare Brandi. 'Il bozzetto di Manzù per la porta di San Pietro'. L'IMMAGINE, Rome, March—April 1949.

162. Anna Maria Brizio. 'Moore e Manzù'. EMPORIUM, Bergamo, May 1949.

163. Cesare Brandi. 'Dal Periplo della scultura moderna: Manzù'. L'IMMAGINE, Rome, May—June 1949.

164. Salvatore Gatto. 'Manzù'. LA FIERA LETTERARIA, Rome, 3 July 1949.

165. Ennio Francia. 'La chiesa romana non respinge le nuove forme del linguaggio d'arte'. IL POPOLO, Rome, 29 July 1949.

166. Fortunato Bellonzi. 'Le porte di San Pietro'. LA FIERA LETTERARIA, Rome, 31 July 1949.

167. Valerio Mariani. 'Le porte di bronzo di S. Pietro'. IDEA, Rome, 31 July 1949.

168. Giovanni Mariacher. 'Manzù e Marini nelle edizioni del Milione'. VERNICE, Trieste, July—December 1949.

169. Attilio Podestà. 'Manzù e la porta di S. Pietro'. EMPORIUM, Bergamo, September 1949.

170. Luciano Bartoli. 'Le porte di S. Pietro'. PALESTRA DEL CLERO, Rovigo, 1 November 1949.

171. Silvano Gianelli. 'Dietro le porte, oltre Manzù'. L'ULTIMA, Florence 1949. No. 47.

172. Italo Faldi. 'Giacomo Manzù'. THE MONTH, London, January 1950.

173. Marco Valsecchi. 'Manzù e le porte di San Pietro'. PANORAMA DELL'ARTE ITALIANA, Turin, January 1950.

174. Marco Valsecchi, 'Chi farà le porte di San Pietro?' LO SMERALDO, Milan, 30 March 1950.

175. Giulio Carlo Argan. 'Difficoltà della scultura'. LETTERATURA—ARTE CONTEMPORANEA. Florence, March—April 1950.

176. Toni Fiedler. 'Neue Bronzetüren für den Petersdom in Rom'. DIE KUNST UND DAS SCHÖNE HEIM, Munich, June 1950.

177. Mario Negri. 'Manzù a Buenos Aires'. DOMUS, Milan, June 1950.

178. Piero Bargellini. 'La Porta di Manzù'. L'OSSERVATORE ROMANO DELLA DOMENICA, Città del Vaticano, 22 October 1950.

179. Carlo Carrà. 'Giacomo Manzù e la porta di San Pietro'. GAZZETTA DI BERGAMO, Bergamo, December 1950—January 1951.

180. Ennio Francia, 'Quattro compiuti capolavori, le stazioni della Via Crucis di Manzù'. IL POPOLO, Rome, 26 July 1951.

181. Fortunato Bellonzi. 'Umanità dell'artista'. LA FIERA LETTERARIA, Rome, 16 September 1951.

182. Nino Bertocchi. 'Manzù, espressione di un dramma italiano'. LA FIERA LETTERARIA, Rome, 16 September 1951.

183. Cesare Brandi. 'Il Paradiso perduto'. LA FIERA LETTERARIA, Rome, 16 September 1951.

184. Carlo Carrà. 'Meditazione, osservazione diretta'. LA FIERA LETTERARIA, Rome, 16 September 1951.

185. Gian Luigi Giovanola. 'Galleria degli artisti italiani: Giacomo Manzù'. LA FIERA LETTERARIA, Rome, 16 September 1951.

186. Giovanni Scheiwiller. 'Inizi di Manzù'. LA FIERA LETTERARIA, Rome, 16 September 1951.

187. Costantino Baroni. 'Giacomo Manzù, scultore della Passione'. IL REGNO, STUDI CRISTIANI, Assisi, January—April 1952.

188. Giovanni Cavicchioli. 'Giacomo Manzù a passo di colomba'. LA FERIA LETTERARIA, Rome, 8 February 1952.

189. Mario Negri. 'Storia di un dramma divino, stazioni di Via Crucis'. DOMUS, Milan, February 1952.

190. Gillo Dorfles. 'Modern Sculpture in Italy'. THE STUDIO, London, October 1952.

191. Gian Luigi Giovanola. 'Giacomo Manzù inedito'. LA FIERA LETTERARIA, Rome, 7 June 1953.

192. Johann Adolf Böck. 'Manzù'. DER GROSSE ENTSCHLUSS, Vienna — Munich, July—August 1954.

193. Max Kaindl-Hönig. 'Kunst — eine Liebe, die sich zu erkennen gibt'. SALZBURGER NACHRICHTEN, Salzburg, 31 July 1954.

194. Heinz Klier. 'Der Mensch, das Mass aller Kunst: zur Ausstellung Kokoschka—Manzù in der Galerie Welz'. DEMOKRATISCHES VOLKSBLATT, Salzburg, 4 August 1954.

195. Wolfgang Schneditz. 'Der Bildhauer Giacomo Manzù. OBERÖSTERREICHISCHE NACHRICHTEN, Linz, 13 August 1954.

196. Karl Maria Grimme. 'Giacomo Manzù'. NEUE TAGESZEITUNG. Vienna, 26 January 1955.

197. Arnulf Neuwirth. 'Manzù im Stubenring-Museum'. WELTPRESSE, Vienna, 27 January 1955.

198. Johann Muschik. 'Manzù oder die Lust am Menschen'. DER ABEND, Vienna, 28 January 1955.

199. Jörg Lampe. 'Manzù: Adel der Wirklichkeit'. DIE PRESSE, Vienna, 29 January 1955.

200. Kurt Moldovan. 'Italiens lächelnder Erbe'. BILD-TELEGRAF, Vienna, 29 January 1955.

201. Wieland Schmied. 'Das Purpurgewand der Kardinäle'. DIE ÖSTERREICHISCHE FURCHE, Vienna, 5 February 1955.

202. Carlo Ludovico Ragghianti. 'Manzù, studio per un ritratto'. CRITICA D'ARTE, Florence, September—November 1955.

203. Giuseppe Scortino. 'Studio per un ritratto'. LA FIERA LETTERARIA, Rome, 25 March 1956.

204. John Maxon. 'Two modern Italian sculptures'. BULLETIN OF THE RHODE ISLAND SCHOOL OF DESIGN. MUSEUM NOTES. Providence, R. I., December 1956.

205. Maria Luisa Gengaro. 'Manzù e la scultura'. ARTE LOMBARDA, Venice—Milan 1956, pp. 132—155.

206. Blida Heynold von Gräfe. 'Manzù und die arte sacra'. DAS MÜNSTER, Munich 1956, No. 9, pp. 156—161.

207. Guido Perocco. 'Manzù per i migliori critici inglesi fa scoprire anche la provincia italiana'. GAZZETTINO SERA, Venice, 4 January 1957.

208. Robert Melville. 'Giacomo Manzù'. THE STUDIO, London, March 1957.

209. 'Giacomo Manzù'. LA BIENNALE DI VENEZIA, Venice, June—September 1957.

210. Jan Tomeš. 'Giacomo Manzù'. VÝTVARNÉ UMĚNÎ, Prague 1957, No. VII.

211. Tito Sansa. 'Giacomo Manzù, anello della Porta di San Pietro'. ROTOSEI SPETTACOLO, Milan, 30 August 1957.

212. Pia Bruzzicheli. 'Opere inedite di Manzù'. LA ROCCA, Assisi, 1 December 1957.

213. Giuseppe Marchiori. 'Scultura Italiana tra due tempi: 1914, 1945, 1956'. QUADRUM, Brussels 1957, III.

214. Marco Varisco. 'Modernità di Manzù'. SGUARDI SUL MONDO, Milan, January–February 1958.

215. Guido Perocco. 'Bianco e nero di Giacomo Manzù'. LA FIERA LETTERARIA, Rome, 25 May 1958.

216. Marco Valsecchi. 'L'evangelario di bronzo di Giacomo Manzù'. IL GIORNO, Milan, 5 July 1958.

217. Ruggero Savinio. 'Mamme e Bambini di Giacomo Manzù'. NOSTRO FIGLIO, Rome, November 1958.

218. 'Giacomo Manzù: Dal bozzetto all'opera compiuta; la porta centrale del Duomo di Salisburgo'. DOMUS, Milan, November 1958.

219. Lionello Venturi. 'The New Painting and Sculpture'. THE ATLANTIC, Boston, December 1958.

220. Lubor Kára. 'Manzù'. VÝTVARNÝ ŽIVOT, Bratislava 1958, No. 4.

221. Giorgio Trentin. 'Mostra di incisioni di Giacomo Manzù'. BOLLETTINO DEI MUSEI CIVICI VENEZIANI, Venice 1958, No. 2.

222. Antonio Manfredi. 'Giacomo Manzù'. COOPERAZIONE, Basel, 29 August 1959.

223. C(arlo) L(udovico) R(agghianti). 'Giacomo Manzù'. SELE ARTE, Florence, September–December 1959.

224. Max Peter Maaß. 'Moderner Bildhauer — ganz konservativ'. DARMSTÄDTER TAGBLATT, Darmstadt, 24 November 1959.

225. K. K. 'Die Manzù-Ausstellung in Frankfurt'. FRANKFURTER ALLGEMEINE ZEITUNG, Frankfurt, 4 December 1959.

226. Elda Fezzi. 'Opinioni sulla scultura di Manzù'. BOLLETTINO DELLA UNIONE STORIA E ARTE, Rome, January–February 1960.

227. 'Manzù'. DOMUS, Milan, March 1960.

228. Cesare Brandi. 'Una Mostra di Manzù a St Gallen'. SEGNACOLO, Bologna, July–August 1960.

229. Lawrence Alloway. 'Fragonard, Mathieu, Manzù'. ART INTERNATIONAL, Zürich, 1 December 1960.

230. Ugo Ferroni. 'Giacomo Manzù'. GOYA, Madrid 1960, No. 35, pp. 292–299.

231. Marcello Camilucci. 'Manzù antico e moderno artefice di armoniosa plastica'. L'OSSERVATORE ROMANO, Città del Vaticano, 16 April 1961.

232. A. Franklin Page. 'Manzù's Bronze Dancer'. BULLETIN OF THE DETROIT INSTITUTE OF ARTS, Detroit, Michigan, 1961, vol. XLI, pp. 10–12.

233. Emilio Lavagnino. 'Manzù artista che non teme di ''apparire'' contro il suo tempo'. IL MESSAGGERO DI ROMA, Rome, 6 January 1962.

234. Mino Borghi. 'Galleria di artisti italiani: Giacomo Manzù'. RIVISTA DELLE PROVINCE, Rome 1962, LIV/12.

235. Maria Grazia Mazzoni. 'L'ultima opera di Manzù e il ritratto di Giovanni XXIII.' SETTIMO GIORNO, Milan, 18 June 1963.

236. Giuseppe Patenè. 'A San Pietro un pavimento di Manzù'. MARMO, RIVISTA INTERNAZIONALE D'ARTE E D'ARCHITETTURA, Milan, October 1963.

237. Marcello Venturolli. 'L'Arte di Giacomo Manzù'. SEGNACOLO, Bologna, November-December 1963.

238. Jules Perahim. 'Giacomo Manzù'. ARTA PLASTICA, Bucharest 1963, No. 12.

239. Blida Heynold von Gräfe. 'St Peters neue Bronzepforten von Manzù'. WELTKUNST, Munich, 1 August 1964.

240. Gio Ponti. 'La porta di Manzù'. DOMUS, Milan, October 1964.

241. Vittorio Rubin. 'L'opera grafica di Manzù'. IL PUNTO, Rome, 21 November 1964.

242. Hélène Demoriane. 'Vatican: la nouvelle porte sculptée par Manzù, témoin du Concile du XXe siècle et de l'art actuel en Saint-Pierre de Rome'. CONNAISSANCE DES ARTS, Paris, December 1964.

243. Giovanni Scheiwiller. 'Manzù'. SEGNALAZIONI — SCRITTI D'ARTE, Milan 1964, pp. 109–20.

244. Marisa Volpi. 'La porta di S. Pietro di Giacomo Manzù'. LA BIENNALE DI VENEZIA, Venice 1964, No. 55, pp. 45–6.

245. Alexander Elliot. 'Manzù. Mason and God'. ART IN AMERICA, New York 1965, No. 53, pp. 130–135.

246. Peter H. Feist. 'Triumph des Realismus — Giacomo Manzùs Tür für den Petersdom in Rom'. BILDENDE KUNST, Berlin 1965, pp. 148–151.

WORKS IN PUBLIC PLACES

1. Weathercock, chased copper, 15¾", 1931. Università Cattolica, Milan

2. Four Saints, relief in granite, 43¼", 1932. Università Cattolica, Milan

3. Heart of Jesus, bas-relief in marble, 47¼", 1933. Assisi

4. History of the Calvi brothers, bas-relief on their monument in Bergamo, marble, l. 29½", 1933

5. St John, bronze, 13¾", 1935. Santa Maria in Chiesa Rossa, Milan

6. The Saints: Charles Borromeo, Ambrose, Benedict and Blasius, Christ and the suffering Mother of God, bronze, 51", 1949. Motta chapel in the Milan cemetery

7. Four Stations of the Cross (XI—XIV), reliefs in bronze, 51", 1950. Church of St Eugenio, Rome

8. Crucifixion, relief in bronze, 59", 1951. Middelheimpark, Antwerp

9. Deposition, relief in bronze, 59", 1951. Middelheimpark, Antwerp

10. Dance Step, bronze, 65", 1951. Middelheimpark, Antwerp

11. Cardinal, bronze, 69", 1952. Middelheimpark, Antwerp

12. Young Girl Playing, bronze, 19¾", 1953. Schulsiedlung, Wiesbaden

13. Cardinal Giacomo Lercaro, bronze, 104", 1953. Basilica S. Petronio, Bologna

14. Cardinal, bronze, 65", 1954. Municipality of Tilburg, Netherlands

15. Dancer, bronze, 80¾", 1956. Municipality of Helmend, Netherlands

16. Ice Skater, bronze, 86¾", 1957. Municipality of Antwerp

17. Ice Skater, bronze, 1958. Stadtsparkasse, Frankfurt am Main

18. Portal of Love, bronze, 186¾" (without frame), w. 92¾", 1958. Salzburg Cathedral

19. Portrait of Inge, bronze, 23¾", 1960. In a department store in the centre of Tokyo

20. Bust of Pope John XXIII, bronze, 25½", 1962. St Mark's, Venice

21. Dance Step, bronze, 134", 1962. Fountain figure in front of the Gas Company building, Detroit

22. Dance Step, bronze, 86½", 1963. Municipality of Darmstadt

23. Door Frame, relief, 1963. Rockefeller Center (Italian Building), New York

24. Portal of Death, 301" (without frame), w. 143¾", 1964. St Peter's, Vatican, Rome

WORKS OWNED BY MUSEUMS

1. Woman Combing Her Hair, bronze, 19¾", 1935. Galleria Nazionale d'Arte Moderna, Rome

2. Susanna, wax, 13¾", 1937. Galleria Nazionale d'Arte Moderna, Rome

3. Cardinal, bronze, 13¾", 1937—8. Galleria Nazionale d'Arte Moderna, Rome

4. Portrait of Rosy Birolli, wax, 6¼", 1938. Museo Civico, Turin

5. Silvia, marble, 8¾", 1938. Moderne Galerie, Budapest

6. Carla, wax bust, 21½", 1940. Galleria Nazionale d'Arte Moderna, Rome

7. Portrait of the Artist's Niece, wax, 7⅛", 1941. Museo Nazionale, Palermo

8. Girl on a Chair, lead, 47¼", 1947. Museo Civico, Turin

9. Child with Duck, bronze, 19¾", 1947. Museo Revoltella, Trieste

10. Cardinal, bronze, 13¾", 1948. Tate Gallery, London

11. Cardinal, bronze, 21½", 1950. Nationalmuseum, Oslo

12. Girl Playing, bronze, 24½", 1943—51. The City Art Gallery, Bristol

13. Cardinal, bronze, 21½", 1951. Museu de Arte Moderna, São Paulo

14. Reclining Woman, bronze, l. 82½", 1942—53. Tate Gallery, London

15. Head of a Woman, bronze, 11", 1953. Koninklijk Museum voor Schone Kunsten, Antwerp

16. Girl on a Chair, bronze, 41¼", 1953. Museo Nacional de Artes Moderno, Madrid

17. Dance Step, bronze, 25½", 1953. Koninklijk Museum voor Schone Kunsten, Antwerp

18. Susanna, bronze, l. 86¾", 1949—54. Civica Galleria d'Arte Moderna, Milan

19. Cardinal, bronze, 65", 1954. Wallraf-Richartz-Museum, Cologne
Variant, Stadthus Tilburg, Holland

20. Dance Step, bronze, 82½", 1954. Städtische Kunsthalle, Mannheim

21. Small Cardinal, bronze, 15½", 1954. Rhode Island School of Design, Providence, U.S.A.

22. Lady in a Dressing Gown, bronze, 65", 1946. Single re-casting, 1955, in the Museum of Modern Art, New York

23. Girl on a Chair, bronze, 41¼", 1955. National Gallery, Toronto, Canada

24. Large Cardinal, bronze, 88½", 1955. Galleria Internazionale d'Arte Moderna, Venice

25. Cardinal, bronze, 39¼", 1965. Civica Galleria d'Arte Moderna, Milan

BIOGRAPHICAL NOTES

1908 Giacomo Manzù born 22 December in Bergamo as the tenth child of a poor cobbler and sexton. Shows early artistic promise. Has to leave school after a few years to learn a trade.

1919–1920 Apprenticed to a wood-carver, where he also works in stone.

1921 Apprenticed to a gilder, then a stucco-worker. Manzù begins to draw, paint and model intensively in his spare time; occasionally attends evening courses at the Fantoni Trade School.

1922 The Fascist March on Rome.

1923 Manzù buys a volume on Maillol in a bookshop in Bergamo; also studies illustrated books about Greek and Roman sculpture, Michelangelo and other artists.

1927 Leaves Bergamo for the first time to do his eighteen months of military service in Verona. He is impressed by the romanesque bronze doors of San Zeno Maggiore and attends the Accademia Cignaroli for a short time. Interest in the art of the film.

1928 Death of Manzù's mother; his first tinted sculptures date from this time.

After release from the army the artist, at the end of the year, goes to Paris where he hopes to meet Maillol and earn enough to devote himself to sculpture exclusively. When his money runs out and he collapses in the street because of hunger, he is deported back to Italy as an undesirable alien. During his stay of 20 days he neither dares to visit Maillol nor has the opportunity to visit the Rodin Museum. After his return home he settles in Milan where Medardo Rosso has died during this year.

1929 The first relief, 'Annunciation', is created in Milan, as well as a series of realistic sculptures, mostly coloured. Manzù meets many young artists and no longer feels quite so isolated.

1930 Manzù obtains his first commission through the architect Muzio: decorating a chapel of the Catholic University. He participates in a group exhibition in Milan and occasionally sells some works, though not enough to escape an oppressive poverty. He draws a great deal and sometimes paints. Influenced by the sculpture of the Egyptians, Etruscans and Minoans, his work shows certain primitive tendencies.

1931 Manzù makes seven drawings of the child of an acquaintance, about eleven years old, which stimulate him two years later to create the 'Girl on a Chair'.

1932 His father dies. Participation in a collective exhibition in the Galleria del Milione in Milan. Giovanni Scheiwiller publishes a monograph about Manzù. Friendship with painters, authors, musicians and art-critics.

1933 The first version of the sitting, naked girl originally with a chair (later removed by the artist), life-size, chased in copper. Tired by the exhausting existence in Milan, Manzù withdraws to Bergamo where he lives in a country house near Selvino and works but little. He devotes himself to painting; also chases some reliefs on religious themes in copper. Pietro Bargellini writes the introduction to an exhibition in Bergamo. The first feminine heads originate in Selvino, showing a certain influence of Medardo Rosso, whom Manzù is beginning to appreciate.

1934 In January, during a short, first visit to Rome, the artist sees the pope sitting between two cardinals in St Peter's; this group impresses him deeply. The first drawing of a 'Cardinal' is done in this year. In Rome he has his first opportunity to study Greek sculptures. Returning to Milan, he marries a young Milanese girl. He continues to create female portrait studies, chiefly in wax, and his first bronzes are cast on credit. Lamberto Vitali and Raffaello Giolli write the preface to an exhibition in Milan. Manzù exhibits for the first time abroad: at St Gallen. The artist destroys many of his works created between 1929 and 1934.

1935 Birth of a daughter. Continuation of a series of feminine heads in wax or bronze. First etchings on the theme 'Painter and Model'. Acquaintance with the poet Quasimodo. The artist begins to make his way; his material position gradually improves.

1936   Mussolini attacks Abyssinia. Manzù undertakes a second trip to Paris, this time accompanied by the painter Aligi Sassù. He stays two weeks, visits the Rodin Museum, briefly meets Lionello Venturi. On their return the two friends smuggle anti-Fascist literature into Italy. Creation of the first sculpture of a cardinal, destroyed by the dissatisfied artist. Manzù exhibits for the first time at the Biennale in Venice.

1937   Birth of a second daughter; both children die the same year. Completely prostrated Manzù goes to Rome for two months. During his absence many of his leftist friends are arrested in Milan; his house is searched but hidden ammunition is not discovered. First one-man show in Rome at the Galleria Cometa, with an introduction by Carlo Carrà, which achieves considerable success. In Rome Manzù becomes acquainted with the art historians Cesare Brandi and Carlo Ragghianti with whom he remains friends to this day. Creation of the first, small high relief of the series 'Painter and Model', of a 'Susanna' in wax and of a twenty-inch high version of the naked 'Girl on a Chair', cast in lead. During 1937 and 1938 the artist again takes up painting.

1938   Manzù attains great success at the Venice Biennale. Creation of 'David' and of a small 'Cardinal' in bronze, the first which satisfies the artist and which inaugurates the future series on this theme. A 'Cardinal' over three feet high in stone follows in the same year. A new series of feminine portraits.

1939   Birth of the artist's son, Pio. Before Hitler attacks Poland and unleashes the Second World War, Manzù is occupied with a series of eight bronze reliefs on the theme 'Cristo nella nostra umanità', which shows a clearly political, anti-Fascist attitude.

1940   Manzù and Carrà, Marini and Casorati are nominated to the Brera in Milan. Manzù is appointed Professor of Sculpture but is 'lent' to the Academy of Turin during the same year. He works on further statues of cardinals and on reliefs, especially on a high relief, 'Self Portrait with Model', a variant of the theme 'Painter and Model'. Ragghianti begins to write a book on Manzù. During the summer Mussolini intervenes in the war. As a teacher at an Academy, Manzù is not liable to conscription.

1941   Teaches in Turin where he becomes acquainted with the painter and author Carlo Levi. During one whole month Manzù works in Rome on numerous drawings and a sculpture of the thirteen-year old Francesca, who also inspires him to do his first 'Dance Step'. The Galleria Barbaroux in Milan exhibits his series of reliefs 'Cristo nella nostra umanità' with an introduction by Cesare Brandi. This brave gesture leads to vigorous polemics.

1942   Manzù teaches in Turin, but later with wife and child withdraws to Clusone, where he sets up a studio. At the Quadrenale in Rome he achieves great success with the bronze of the sitting 'Francesca' and is awarded the Grand Prix. He works on a new relief, 'Painter and Model' and also makes seven etchings on this theme which appear in a book on Manzù published in Milan.

1943   The artist continues to live in Clusone but travels regularly to Milan where he has again taken up his appointment at the Brera. He begins to paint once more. Under the influence of wartime events further reliefs of the 'Crucifixion' series are created in Clusone. The Americans capture Anzio.

1944   Manzù has to leave Clusone by order of the Germans; he hides with a friend in Bergamo. Francesca visits him there. He continues teaching in Milan; he and the director of the Brera are the only ones at the Academy when the Americans arrive in the spring.

1945   The artist and his family return to Milan, where he continues to teach at the Brera for a further ten years. Occupied with the theme of 'Cardinals'. 'Laudi' by Jacopone da Todis is published in Milan with illustrations by Manzù.

1946   The meeting with Signora Alice Lampugnani leads to the great sculpture 'Lady in a Dressing Gown' and a series of nearly one hundred drawings which occupy the artist for two years.

1947   Continuation of work on the sculpture of Signora Lampugnani. Creation of the life-size version of the naked 'Girl on a Chair' (in lead, with the chair cast in bronze). Busy with the 'Child with a Duck'. On 1 July the Vatican announces an international competition for a portal of St Peter's; Manzù decides to compete. A large one-man show at the

Palazzo Reale in Milan, with an introduction by Lionello Venturi, contributes considerably to the renown of the artist.

1948   First model for the portal of St Peter's. Manzù is among the twelve artists, called on by the jury to enter a second competition. At the Venice Biennale Manzù exhibits his works in a room of his own, among them his 'Girl on a Chair'. He receives the prize for Italian sculpture. The artist is further occupied with the theme of 'Cardinals' and also etches illustrations for Virgil's GEORGICS, published by Hoepli in Milan. Greatly impressed by an exhibition of Giovanni Pisano in Pisa.

1949   A brochure about Manzù's project for the portal of St Peter's is published anonymously in Rome; the author is a friend of the artist, Monsignor Giuseppe De Luca. Creation of the first large 'Cardinal', as well as of the first definite version and a variant of the 'Girl on a Chair' in bronze.

1950   Work on four high reliefs of the 'Passion' and on further cardinals. Manzù is one of three sculptors whom the Vatican intends to commission for the portals of St Peter.

1951   Occupied with the 'Dance Step' and the theme of the 'Crucifixion' with which the artist has been preoccupied since 1939.

1952   In January Manzù receives the official commission for new portal of St Peter's dedicated to the 'Triumph of the Saints and Martyrs of the Church'. He participates in a group exhibition at the Hanover Gallery in London. Manzù's wife leaves him; the only surviving child of the marriage, the thirteen-year old Pio, remains in his custody; a legal separation follows later. Makes a new series of drawings of Francesca which are exhibited in Turin, but Manzù destroys them, almost without exception, soon afterwards.

1953   Visits London in connection with his first one-man show abroad, arranged at the Hanover Gallery by Erica Brausen. He is particularly captivated by the Elgin Marbles in the British Museum. Manzù completes the large 'Portrait of Cardinal Lercaro' for Bologna.

1954   Having taught at the Brera for almost fifteen years, Manzù resigns his professorship because the Ministry of Culture rejects his suggestions for a new international school of art. The same year Fried-rich Welz appoints him to the International Summer Academy in Salzburg, where Kokoschka has opened his 'School of Seeing'. Welz simultaneously arranged an exhibition of sculptures and drawings by Manzù and paintings by Kokoschka. In Salzburg he becomes acquainted with a young dancer Inge who becomes his favourite model. He works on portrait busts of Inge, on dance steps and cardinals and completes a reclining 'Susanna' which had occupied him since 1949. Creation of seven lithographs as illustrations for Quasimodo's IL FALSO E VERO VERDE published by Schwarz in Milan. Radical changes of his project for the portal of St Peter's.

1955   Welz arranges a Manzù exhibition in Salzburg, which is subsequently shown in Cologne, Stuttgart, Bremen, Utrecht and Vienna. The artist continues working on the themes of dance steps and cardinals and makes portrait busts of Inge's younger sister Sonja. The last variants of the theme 'Girl on a Chair'. During the summer teaches at Salzburg, where he is asked to submit a design for the doors of the cathedral.

1956   During the preparation for the Salzburg portal the artist is particularly concerned with the theme of 'Mother and Child'. He exhibits some of his cardinals at the Venice Biennale where he obtains international success. Through his friend Monsignor Giuseppe De Luca he becomes acquainted with Angelo Roncalli, the Patriarch of Venice, who hails from Bergamo. Manzù teaches again at Salzburg. Further cardinals, dancers and busts of Inge are made. Toward the end of the year a new exhibition at the Hanover Gallery in London.

1957   First show at the World House Gallery in New York in the spring; introduction to the catalogue by John Rewald. Manzù proposes a new project for an art school in Milan; despite enthusiastic reception and financial support from industry it comes to nothing. During the summer the artist teaches at Salzburg once more and is definitely commissioned to make the portal of the cathedral. From 1957 to 1959 renewed interest in painting, especially in the theme 'Painter and Model'. Meeting with John Rewald in autumn. Creation of the first 'Ice Skater'.

1958   Manzù teaches again in Salzburg, where his portal is inaugurated on 28 June. Welz arranges an exhibition of the studies for this work, to which he also devotes a small book with preface by Franz Fuhrmann. Further busts of Inge; Sonja poses for an 'Ice Skater'. Manzù moves from Milan to Rome to work on the portal of St Peter's. After the death of Pius XII, the Patriarch of Venice, whom Manzù had met through Monsignor De Luca, is elected pope. Manzù is honoured with the official commission for a bust of the new pope, John XXIII.

1959   Teaching in Salzburg. New busts of Inge, ice-skaters and studies on the theme 'Painter and Model'. Creation of the last 'Cardinal'. Towards the end of the year Glauco Pellegrini starts to make a documentary film about Manzù's work on the portal of St Peter's. In the summer Welz organizes a great, European travelling exhibition of Manzù's work starting at the Haus der Kunst in Munich, which reaches the Historische Museum in Frankfurt-am-Main in autumn,

1960   and the Nationalgalerie in Berlin in 1960. Subsequently displayed at the Ateneum in Helsinki. During the summer, partially installed in the open and enriched by many new works shown in Zwerglgarten in Salzburg and finally at the Tate Gallery in London. This is the last year in which the artist teaches at Salzburg; on the suggestion of Friedrich Welz he models a portrait of Oskar Kokoschka. Second exhibition at the World House Gallery in New York. From 1960 to 1962 the artist works on the bust of John XXIII.

1961   Manzù visits New York in March and spends a few days in Detroit where, through the architect Yamasaki, he receives two commissions for fountains. While working on the bust of John XXIII he obtains papal permission to change the general theme for the portal of St Peter's. It now becomes a 'Portal of Death'; this produces further extensive changes in the project.

1962   In February John XXIII calls a second council for the autumn; Manzù designs an inscribed emblem which is let into the floor of St Peter's. Monsignor De Luca dies. Exhibition of drawings in Salzburg, arranged by Welz, and in the Palazzo della Pinacoteca in Bergamo. The actual work on the portal of St Peter's begins.

1963   Despite transitory illness Manzù works on the portal for St Peter's during the whole year. He decides to settle outside Rome. John XXIII dies on 3 June and Manzù is commissioned to cast the death-mask.

1964   The portal of St Peter's is inaugurated on 28 June by Paul VI. Completion of a standing 'Dancer' for the fountain in Detroit. Variants of the reliefs for the portal of St Peter's are exhibited at the Sala Napoleone in Venice. A catalogue of the graphic works of Manzù with an introduction by Carlo L. Ragghianti is published by Nuova Pesa in Rome. On 15 October the artist moves into his new house near Ardea. An exhibition of paintings of the series 'Painter and Model' is shown at the Galleria d'Arte Contemporanea in Turin from the end of 1964 until early 1965.

1965   Short visit to Picasso in the spring. The series of paintings 'Painter and Model' is exhibited in the Hanover Gallery, London. A relief of a 'Mother and Child' is installed at Rockefeller Center, New York. Preoccupation with the new themes 'Pair of Lovers' and 'Striptease'. Project for a church portal in Rotterdam. Variants of the reliefs for the portal of St Peter's exhibited at Paul Rosenberg Gallery, New York.

1966   Manzù receives the International Lenin Peace Prize. Journey to Rotterdam and signing of the contract for the portal of the Sankt-Laurents Church. Exhibition of the reliefs for the 'Portal of Death' and variants on the theme 'Cristo nella nostra umanità' at the Galerie Welz in Salzburg.